Colorado City History
Through the Eyes of the Iris

By Suzanne Schorsch

Old Colorado City Historical Society Publishing

Published by
the Old Colorado City Historical Society

Published in the United States of America
by the
Old Colorado City Historical Society
1 South 24th Street, Colorado Springs, Colorado 80904

Schorsch, Suzanne M.

COLORADO CITY HISTORY
THROUGH THE EYES OF THE IRIS
1st edition:

ISBN# 978-0-9839952-6-5

PRINTED IN THE UNITED STATES OF AMERICA

Cover design, book design/layout by Suzanne Schorsch and Donald R. Kallaus

Dedication

To all historians from the Old Colorado City Historical Society who researched the history of a very colorful city, to the town's old-timers who have given so many items to the History Center connecting us to the residents long gone, and to Pikes Peak Library Special Collection for preserving newspapers that have given us a glimpse of the past, thank you so very much. To Roberta Hardy, who helped me immensely, thank you. Most importantly, to Tom, my husband, for letting me spend my time researching history and supporting me in so many ways.

Special recognition to those friends and members of OCCHS who's research over the years was invaluable to this book: Merv Casey, Peggy Dougherty, Catherine Dymkoski, Don Ellis, Roberta Hardy, Dave Hughes, Leo Knudson, Jan Knox, Marvie Randall, Paul Shepard, and Sharon Swint.

A house divided against itself cannot stand. Abraham Lincoln's speech given in 1858 foreshadowed the dividing of a country. It was also applicable for Colorado City, founded one year later. A city divided will also crumble. Colorado City at the turn of the 19th century was a city divided: alcohol or prohibition, annexation or independent city. Circumstances would divide it in half, not only on issues, but on the location certain businesses would be allowed and the type of businesses desired. The south side of Colorado Avenue would contain saloons, brothels and gambling halls. The north side of Colorado Avenue would contain family businesses, churches and the library. This was not how it was when Colorado City began, but it was how divisions shaped the city at its end.

Table of Contents

THE BEGINNINGS

Big Dreams – Small Town

Colorado City was founded in August 1859 by the Colorado City Town Company, a group of investors including, Bott, Bute, Gilmore, Winchester, Price, Beach, Tappan, Witsett, Parke, McClure, Waggoner and Sheldon. Melancthon Beach and Rufus Cable were sent to stake claim to the 1,280 acres east of a pass the Ute Indians used as a route to the mountains. These investors believed that Colorado City, with easy mountain access, would be the gateway to the mountains for gold prospectors. Prior attempts had been made to settle the area, but Colorado City became the first permanent settlement in the Pikes Peak Region. The investors had dreams that the town would become an important supply town for miners. Although early reports told of many people, businesses and homes built in the area, most reports, along with the description of Colorado City found on the original Fosdick Plat, were marketing tools for the hopeful Town Company to lure people and investors to the area.

The Town Company hired Henry Fosdick, a Harvard engineering graduate, to lay-out and plat the city. It was legally recorded in December 1859. The plat of Colorado City was then lithographed by the Miesel Brothers in Boston. The plat not only showed the lay-out of

Sounds promising? Think how people felt when they arrived at this booming city. A more accurate description would be one found in the diary of Henry Fosdick's daughter. A copy was given to the Old Colorado City Historical Society by the descendants of the Fosdick family. Lucy kept a diary when Henry moved his family to the area. Lucy Fosdick wrote the following:

> Here on May 10th 1861, we unloaded our goods, and set up our primitive housekeeping. The town consisted of one street, with a store and a few other houses at the other end from where we lived. A desolate and forlorn place it must have appeared to my mother, coming from the luxuries of a New England life.

This was not the only time a description of an area was exaggerated for marketing reasons. One of the earliest pioneer families to the area, which would become the State of Colorado, was the Gehrung family. The Gehrung family came west to set up a business in Denver in the 1860s. They had read in a newspaper that the area was a "Grand City." According to family members that still reside in Colorado, upon arrival, the matriarch of the family, Elizabeth, was noted as saying:

> We got there and I thought that there was some mistake, as we heard it was a grand city and all we saw were tents.

The Gehrung family would open a supply store in Colorado City in 1868. The *Rocky Mountain News* of January 27, 1868, wrote about the "dull" town of Colorado City but gave credit to Emile Gehrung and the new building that would house the Pioneer Store:

> Colorado City is somewhat dull, yet the people are generally hopeful. The houses are all occupied by either permanent or

temporary citizens. The later class is mostly from the mining locality to the west who come down to spend the winter and send their children to school.... Some new houses have been erected this past season. Among the most notable is a fine stone storeroom 80x60 built by the Messrs. Gehrung formerly of Denver. The front is of finely cut stone, and the whole building would reflect credit upon the town.

The Gehrung stone store hand drawn by Emile Gehrung in 1878. (Drawing from Peggy Dougherty, descendent of the Gehrung family, used with permission)

An article in the *Colorado Springs Gazette* on September 20, 1906, looked back at the early days of Colorado City. It reported that in 1859 Albert Richardson rode on horseback from Taos, New Mexico, researching his book *Beyond the Mississippi*. Later, in the published book, Richardson wrote the following:

October 8, journeyed up the Fountaine Qui Bouille directly toward Pike's Peak, which, with its dark wood sides and irregular turreted summit, towers far above all adjacent mountains. Plump antelopes abounded so tame that when I stopped my pony a long herd of one hundred and twenty in single file crossed the path before me, within a stone's throw. Just before dark in the gigantic shadow of Pike's Peak, I reached a little sign board labeled 'Colorado Avenue.' I had not seen a single human being since morning, and the idea of a city in those solitudes savored on ludicrous; but there it stood, unmistakable evidence of civilization and speculation.

On October 3, 1946, the *Colorado Springs Independent,* carried this excerpt from a newspaper, *The Missouri Democrat,* written in the March 20, 1860 issue by Professor Goldrick:

Colorado City, Foot of Pikes Peak, El Paso County, Jefferson Territory, March 1, 1860. This is destined to be second to no city in the great Territory of Jefferson. Good city property here I consider as valuable as in Denver City. Choice lots here on Broadway Street are worth $500 to $1,000. It is situated at the great natural opening of Ute Pass from the plains to the parks and all other regions in the gold regions west of Utah…There are now some 240, fine, handsome looking houses erected and hundreds more in process of being erected. Some very large, three-story stone store-houses and some very handsome Gothic offices and dwellings are completing.

This quote is very interesting as the first lumber mill arrived in 1860 and early photography taken in the late 1860s shows no sign of the three-story stone store-houses let alone Gothic offices and dwellings.

The truth of the appearance of Colorado City in those early days will lie somewhere between the reports used for marketing and diaries kept at the time. Even the newspaper felt that Professor Goldrick might be the origins of the term 'goldbrick.' A goldbrick was a term used for a brick covered in gold so that the owner could make gain. The brick was all but worthless, pretending to be of value.

Colorado became a territory in 1861 and Colorado City became the Territorial Capitol, but after meeting three days, with lack of accommodations, (where were all those reported buildings?) it was moved to Denver. The *Colorado Springs Gazette* in 1906 reported the law required the new governor and secretary reside in the Territorial Capital. Governor Evans, however, had invested his money in Denver real estate. He did not wish to move to Colorado City.

El Paso County's first school was built in Colorado City in 1861. The first flour mill was built in 1862. The first lumber mill in the area was the Finley Sawmill located north of Colorado City in what is now known as the Black Forest. City founder Anthony Bott and his brother-in-law, John Langmeyer owned the local quarry.

The Civil War, along with Indian troubles, stopped the growth of Colorado City, but only for a short time. During the Indian troubles of 1868, Colorado City residents gathered at the Anway Hotel, one of the safest structures in town. The Anway was a two-story small log structure that the town erected log pickets around for safety. This hotel still stands today and is a small home on Pikes Peak Avenue. The log pickets are gone and the log cabin has been covered with siding. A historic plaque marks the spot.

By the 1870s Colorado Springs and Manitou Springs were founded. Colorado City was almost a dream that had died. A brief history found in *The Rocky Mountain Directory and Colorado Gazetteer for 1871* described the town of Colorado City:

A great many enterprising men, with capital, located at Colorado City for the purpose of opening a permanent field for business operations, and for a time the town flourished, and was indeed the most promising place for the metropolis of the Territory; but soon a series of adversities reduced it to what it now remains, a small, deserted country village, dependent entirely upon farm produce. Among the principal causes of its decline was the discovery of the Gregory gold mines, in Gilpin county, to which Denver was the nearest market; the opening of the Ben Halladay stage line, with general offices at Denver, and the frequent Indian outbreaks along the Arkansas route, left unprotected.

Colorado City from a distance taken around 1868.
(OCCHS Archives, McKnight Collection)

The book *Colorado, Its Gold and Silver Mines, Farms and Stock Ranges and Heath and Pleasure Resorts a Tourist Guide to the Rocky*

Mountains by Frank Fossett written in 1879 describes Colorado City as follows:

> *Small village, between Colorado Springs and Manitou and two miles from the former. Population 100. Daily mail, express and hacks from railroad. In early times was for a very short period designated as the capital of the territory.*

When the Colorado Midland Railroad was organized in 1883 and later gold was discovered in Cripple Creek, Colorado City had a rebirth. It became the working man's town with factories, mills, repair shops for the Midland and a quarry. Colorado City finally struck gold. But it was a different kind. It came in a mug and had foam on the top. Beer! Colorado Springs allowed no alcohol. Colorado City became famous for its many saloons frequented by those from the growing Colorado Springs and miners passing through on their way to the gold fields. With the saloons came brothels and gambling.

Early settlers included farmers, ranchers, freighters and outfitters for the people rushing west to find gold or a new life. By 1886 the Colorado Midland Railroad was one of the city's largest employers, with its headquarters, offices, a terminal and repair yards in Colorado City.

A. STOCKBRIDGE,
— WHOLESALE —
WINE AND LIQUOR
MERCHANT.
Manufacturer of Soda, Ginger Ale, Champagne Cider, etc.
Cheapest House in the State for Cigars.
County Agent for CAMEO Cigarette.
Milwaukee, Golden and Denver
BEER.
The largest stock in the west and prices the lowest for the quality of goods. I will sell lower than Denver houses, and give in the freight!
OFFICE & WAREHOUSE—Colorado Avenue and Third street,
Colorado City, · · · · Colorado.

The Colorado City Glass Works was opened in 1889 in the new Bott Addition of Colorado City. Bohemian glass blowers who came to the area made bottles for Manitou mineral water, liquor and wine. Anheuser-Busch, Charles Stockbridge along with others bottled beer in Colorado City, with the glass works producing over 100 bottles a day. By 1891, the glass works were employing 200 workers.

Gold ore reduction mills were built near Colorado City to process Cripple Creek Gold. The Colorado-Philadelphia built in 1896, the Portland and Telluride Mills built in 1900, the Standard Mill in 1901 and the Golden Cycle Mill in 1908, brought prosperity to the city. Available work brought immigrants with families. Colorado City would be reported in the paper as The Payroll Town.

Yes, Colorado City had its wild side, but most of the residents were hard working families, proud of their schools, Carnegie library and churches. Colorado City had its opera house, holiday parades, the Midland Band and all the societies and clubs that a large eastern city would have, not forgetting the Women's Improvement Society and the Women's Christian Temperance Union.

Colorado City residents took the Midland Flower Excursion.
(OCCHS Archives)

THE SOUTH SIDE

Successful Saloons

Colorado City in the late 1890s and early 1900s was known for its many saloons. Business directories show names such as the Little Gem Club, the Office Club, the Nickel Plate and the Arcade. Each year new saloons would be added and some would disappear. One of the longest lasting saloons was the Oxford, later called the Oxford Club.

Directories of businesses and people living in Colorado City were sometimes inaccurate or incomplete; often listing only the name of the saloon, other times only listing the proprietor. Earlier directories would give the street name, without number addresses, for the location of a business. Some would only put what "block" the Colorado Avenue business was located. The number system for addresses also changed in Colorado City. One way to find out what saloons were located in Colorado City and were successful is to look at the size and number of advertisements the owners placed in the local paper, such as *The Iris*.

In the 1880s, saloons, hotels with bars and gentlemen's club were proudly looked at as businesses good for the economy and their owners as a successful part of the Colorado City community. The local newspaper *The Iris* would run sketches, or brief stories, on the businessmen who owned these businesses. Advertisements and stories of the time show that not all places that sold liquor in Colorado City were the wild saloons that many today believe, some were places for the upper class to be entertained while others were family businesses. Below are stories that were featured in *The Iris* September 27, 1895, on two of the more successful drinking establishments.

The Hoffman Club: 502-508 Colorado Avenue

THE HOFFMAN.

508 COLORADO AVE.

Constantly on Hand the Best Brands of Liquors—
Wholesale and Retail.

**ALSO AGENT FOR THE CELEBRATED
ANHEUSER-BUSCH BEER.**

N. B. HAMES, Proprietor.

The Hoffman Club, has since April 1887 been a vigorous and popular factor in the circles of amusement and pastime in Colorado City, second indeed to none in its sphere, south of Denver. This house pioneered in making this place a resort to pass time and pleasure in these parts, and in truth to the energy, acumen and public spirits of its chief guiding spirit, N.B. Hames, the town is not little indebted for its present day of prominence and prosperity. For this gentleman has ever made the promotion of Colorado City's welfare a part of his private policy and with disinterested devotion, to the town of his home has advanced its interests as he has advanced his own. What he has done for Colorado City, the Hoffman Hotel, *costing $25,000 and the building that envelops this merry retreat, costing $10,000 both architectural trophies beautifying the place, eloquently voice the progressive spirit of the man. Furnished in polished cherry, his resplendent retreat is the Hoffman House bar and a Monte Carlo in miniature wedded. French plate mirrors multiply the enchantment of the resort and the handsome young men who dispense its hospitality. George M. Geiss, the manager for five years, has made hosts of friends for the house, and although young has for twelve years been serenely skillful in this vocation. A general favorite with the public is John Bland, the elegant and suave entertainer who makes every patron a friend. Of Mr. Hames, it is his due, that what Colorado City is today, such as he has made it and its hopes and its destiny is invested in such strong hands liberal, but modest proverbially man as he is.* F.W.Ellis*

The Iris article on the Hotel Hoffman described the two-story brick establishment which opened in 1894 with thirty rooms. Mrs. Hames was in charge of household affairs and made the place feel like home. It was hailed as a public necessity as, according to the article, there was no place prior to that time that offered "elegant entertainment." The article continued stating the hotel filled the demands of the most fastidious:

The rooms are inviting to the wearied one, their every meal is a Belshazzar feast.

It can be wondered why the newspaper called the meal a Belshazzar feast. Belshazzar was the son of the last Babylonian king. It is written he held a grand feast with only the best, but handwriting appeared on the wall letting Belshazzar know he had blasphemed against God, and his kingdom would be given to others. For the Hotel Hoffman to hold a meal called a Belshazzar feast seems pretty accurate when finding out the end for Mr. Hames.

Advertisements in 1895 for the Hotel Hoffman, located at the corner of Colorado Avenue and West Street, stated hotel rates were $2 and $2.50 per day with special rates for regular guests.

In August of 1895 there was a ball held at the Hoffman. The newspaper reported Mr. and Mrs. Hames held the affair at the Hotel Hoffman for their friends. The grand ball ended with a banquet:

> *The guests who comprised the best people of our city, began to arrive early. They thronged the spacious parlors, halls and engaged in conversations until Guerrieri's Italian Orchestra, of Denver, began to tune their instruments in the large dining room on the ground floor, which was a signal that dancing was in order. The Iris continued: The great room was alight as electric lights could make it and the floor was filled with ladies and gentlemen clad in garments appropriate for the occasion. It was indeed an assembly of handsome men and fair women.*

Dinner was served at 12 o'clock. The tables were decorated with pink and white flowers and laden with fruit. The guest register shows more than one hundred were present. This in no way paints the picture of a bawdy event. How attitudes would change a few years later.

In December of 1896, the Hotel Hoffman offered a Christmas Dinner served from five o'clock until eight. Santa Claus was in attendance and everyone was presented with a fine gift. Shown is the menu in full, as printed in the paper. It is highly unusual. There seems to be a political flavor to the meal that I would love to understand.

Hotel Hoffman
Xmas Dinner 1896
Menu
New York Counts, al la Lombard Street
Celery, Nerve Food a la Colorado
Consommé a la U.S. Customs receipts and Treasury Gold Reserve
Olives, Kuner's Pickles a la Cabinet, Radishes

———

Gold fish Flounders a la Bond Issue

———

Roast Ox, White House Style, Runcoed a la Wall Street
(Colorado Springs Packing Company)
Baked Spring Chicken, Silver Dressing a la 16 to 1

———

Golden Succotash a la Sucker Stock, Auriferous Potato Chips
Baked Sweet Potatoes a la Jersey City

———

Fricasseed Canvasback Duck, Bond Syndicate Stuffing
Lamb Cutlets, Breaded Milanese
Golden Grape Jelly, Grand Junction

———

Lettuce a la Greenback

———

Ice Cream a la Pikes Peak
Real English Pudding a la Tariff Reform
Cream Pie a la Boston, Blueberry Pie
California Select Fruit
National Crackers a la "Cousin Ed"
Gold Brand Cream Cheese, Ft. Collins

———

English Breakfast and Green Tea
Milk, Denver Roasted Coffee,
SEATS RESERVED UPON APPLICATION

In the *Portrait and Biographical Record*, a book containing leading citizens in Colorado published in 1898, it stated Noel Byron Hames was the "father" of the town. When he came to Colorado City there was one running stage between the Springs and Colorado City, but soon, according to the book, there were thirteen hacks followed by a line of street cars. Not only did Hames own the Hoffman, but also a private bank which cashed pay checks for the Midland Railroad Company.

The *Colorado City Argus (The Argus)* of November 31, 1911, reported the death of N.B. Hames's only living son, Gus, who had passed away in October. It stated that the family moved to Colorado City around 1887. *The Argus* also reported Mr. Hames, known for his charity work in Colorado City, was collecting supplies for the suffering farmers in the eastern part of El Paso County. Although Hames knew financial ups and downs in his life, he was known to always give to others and was highly respected.

Mr. Hames, whose father had died during the Civil War from wounds received in battle, left the family farm in Illinois to make his fortune in Colorado. Byron married Vesta Viola and had two children. He was a successful gambler and money he made was invested in real estate and his businesses. The "Local" section of *The Iris* on August 13th, 1892, reported the following:

> *The Hoffman is being carpeted in fine style. We hear that Byron (Mr. Hames) made a winning at a Colorado Springs horserace the other day that foots the bill and leaves a neat balance.*

One story told about Mr. Hames was very prophetic. The newspaper was warning the public regarding the gypsies that camped west of Colorado City along Fountain Creek in the summer. The gypsy fortune tellers would rid summer visitors of their money. One such fortune teller told Mr. Hames that he would end his life on the street as an evangelist. Mr. Hames had been noted as having purchased several hymnals, possibly for a church, but because of the gypsy's story, the newspaper wondered, jokingly, if Mr. Hames would need the books later in life when he was living as an evangelist.

Being known as the father of Colorado City was an appropriate title for Mr. Hames. Like most fathers, he loved his children, the residents of Colorado City, both good and bad. He would pay bail for some of the soiled doves on occasion, knowing that many of the girls were not bad women, just living in hard times. Gus, Byron's son, married a soiled dove.

One article in the *Gazette* reported that when a prior marshal from Colorado City, Pete Eales, was arrested while working for law enforcement in Cripple Creek, Hames put up bail of $1,000. Unfortunately, Eales skipped town and Hames was out the money. Later Eales would write to Hames stating he wanted to come back to Colorado City and make things right, if Hames would send him train fare. Hames provided the money, but Eales never came back.

According to his wife, Mr. Hames made a lot, spent a lot and gave much away to charity. When Colorado City voted dry his property was heavily mortgaged and he moved his saloon business to the newly formed town of Ramona. Then when the State of Colorado went dry, the family lost their property and had to sell off their furniture. Things went from bad to worse and his wife left him and went to California.

In January of 1916, *The Colorado City Independent* ran an article "Some Real Tragedies" reporting Bryan Hames was leaving Colorado City. It reported Hames was seen walking down Fourth Street (today's 24th Street), an old man past the middle days of his life. He was carrying a broom over one shoulder with a grip in one hand and another across the broom handle. The article continued reporting that Hames, who at one time could write a check for any amount and have it honored, said of his two cases, they held his entire savings of his lifetime. He left Colorado City with the few things he had left. The article continued as follows:

This man is honest to a fault. Kind, generous, ever ready to help in the face of such awful losses he has retained a disposition to be envied in many ways.

The Independent wished Byron Hames good luck where ever he went. Mr. Hames relied on charity until he died. The local Eagle lodge paid for his burial in his family plot. We don't know if he was living on the streets, but he was destitute. The block that contained the Hoffman saloon, hotel, pool hall and restaurant was torn down to build a strip mall.

The Hiawatha Branch: A Public Resort for Gentlemen
510 Colorado Avenue

In September of 1895 a branch of the Hiawatha Club, a club in the nearby town of Manitou in business starting in 1890, opened in Colorado City. The Hiawatha Club in Manitou was known world over as the town of Manitou was a tourist destination. The Colorado City branch located on the south side of Colorado Avenue at 510 Colorado Avenue (the 2500 block today) became an instant success with hundreds flocking in, according to the newspaper, to partake in its palatial quarters, the purest and most palatable wares and handsome impartial treatment of customers.

The paper reported the Hiawatha Branch was owned by F. Smith and C. Hallenbeck, both known as progressive businessmen with crystal integrity. It was also reported the community was to be congratulated on the aquistion of such men. This is a prime example of how the values at the turn of the century would change drastically. Businessmen who owned drinking establishments would go from an asset to the community to being looked down upon.

Advertising for the Hiawatha Branch Saloon and club rooms stated they sold seven-year-old W.H. McBryer Sour Mash Whiskey, first-class liquors, standard wines and imported cigars. It also boasted a free exhibition of Relfsky's painting, "A Glimpse of the Harem." According to the newspaper, the painting was said to be:

... a masterpiece of art showing a paragon of beauty whose eyes are eloquent in their life like realism, sight of it ravishes the eye, she is bewitchingly beautiful.

Relfsky was a Russian painter who exhibited at world fairs and expositions in the late 1800s with shows in Paris, Vienna, Philadelphia and Chicago. It seems harem life was something those from the west found interesting in the 1800s.

Colorado City Beer Hall – A Family Man's Bar

The Schmidt family moved to Colorado City in 1888. In 1890, Jacob Schmidt was listed as residing in Colorado City as a baker. By 1896 he had gone into business with Louie Rump and opened a saloon at 612 Colorado Ave, the 2600 block today. Schmidt bought out Rump and in 1910 built a new brick building on his property next to the original saloon. That building still stands. Called the Colorado City Beer Hall, within the building was the family delicatessen and bakery. Advertisements were almost daily in the newspaper expounding on the excellence of the bakery. Jacob Schmidt was one example showing a good family man could be in the saloon business.

Jacob's wife, Bertha, a member of the Woman's Christian Temperance Union, detested drinking. Bertha was Jacobs's business partner and a successful businesswomen herself. She was not involved with the saloon but ran the other family enterprises. By 1904 the Schmidts had added a "genteel area" for families to eat while their husbands had a beer elsewhere in the building. As a family establishment the Schmidts posted a sign within the building stating that no bawdy house inmates or fast women of any description were allowed to make purchase in the establishment.

Schmidt maintained the saloon as well as the Zang Brewing Company until prohibition. Trying to stay afloat, Jacob supplemented their income with a produce and fruit stand.

First Colorado City Beer Hall, with Jacob Schmidt standing by the door with his hands on his hips, located at 612 Colorado Avenue. (OCCHS Archives, Schmidt Collection)

The Schmidts had a beautiful home on Colorado Avenue for their family. They were active in the community. When looking at names who donated to charitable causes around Colorado City, Jacob Schmidt was usually on that list. When Colorado City went dry, Jacob invested in an orchard. Unfortunately, making a living with the orchard was not lucrative and Jacob committed suicide. His death notice printed in the paper stated that Jacob had been despondent from the time when "old town" went dry.

Jacob and Bertha had four children; the fourth died in infancy and their second died at the age of seven. Their daughter, Louisa, was born in Colorado City on December 24, 1890. A family story relayed was that Bertha delivered her daughter, Louisa, on Christmas Eve, and then went to work the next day to accommodate walk-in customers. Their children, Henry and Louisa, lived full and productive lives.

Jacob and Bertha's descendants are one of the families that have given photographs and family research to the Old Colorado City Historical Society, allowing future generations to learn of the lives of those families that were part of Colorado City.

The Schmidt home on Colorado Avenue.
(OCCHS Archives, Schmidt Collection)

The Colorado City Beer Hall as it stands today on Colorado Avenue.
(OCCHS Archives, Schmidt Collection)

Jacob Schmidt behind the bar.
(OCCHS Archives, Schmidt Collection)

The Oxford and the Question of Tunnels

We know that T. J. Matthews was listed as a saloon keeper in Colorado City as early as 1890. Matthews was the known manager for The Oxford for many years. In the early 1890s The Oxford, one of the most successful saloons in the city, was owned by Z.S. Brown Mercantile Company with Matthews as Manager.

THE—
OXFORD
Bar, Billiard and Pool
ROOM.

Old Post Office Stand, 504 Colorado Avenue.

The only house in El Paso County that keeps one brand for everybody—one price to all. The best line of Bottled Goods for Families.

T. J. MATTHEWS,   Z. S. BROWN & CO.
Manager,   Proprietors.

Advertisements for The Oxford ran on the front page, center, on almost every issue of *The Iris* during 1892. It was located at 504

Colorado Avenue at the old Post Office Stand. Its advertisement boasted the following:

> The only house in El Paso County that keeps one brand for everybody – one price for all. The best line of bottled goods for families. .

The Oxford Club was in the news September 3, 1892, with the announcement:

> A 'Special Wire' has been put into the Oxford by Western Union Telegraph Company and an 'Operator' detailed to receive the results of fights just two seconds after each round as seen live in New Orleans! Even while the gladiator's blows yet echo through the club house at New Orleans.

The Oxford management, still T.J. Matthews, reminded readers:

> Don't fail to be on hand and learn the results of the great battles, round by round.

By 1893, The Oxford still was running ads on the front page, but they now boasted being the largest house in the County with everything first-class. It had a bar along with billiard and pool rooms. Advertising then showed a picture of The Oxford on the south side of Colorado Avenue. The Oxford would continue to grow.

The biggest local news story on February 3, 1894 was the Grand Opening of the new Oxford Club. The new location of the Oxford Club was on the corner of Colorado Avenue and West Street. That location and address, when it was built, was known as the Templeton Building in the Templeton Block. *The Iris* reported the Oxford Club as follows:

> *One of the most elegant and complete resorts in the Rocky Mountain region. The opening will happen tonight when prominent gentlemen from Leadville, Pueblo, Denver, Cripple Creek and Colorado Springs will be present.*

Although most saloons were on the south side of Colorado Avenue with brothels one block further south, we know that The Oxford Club had moved to the north side of the street, and into the building that was built for Henry Templeton. The Templeton Building was completed in 1891 for $15,000 by contractor Albert Allen.

When the town's upstanding citizens were attempting to keep that which was unsavory on the south side of Colorado Avenue, moving a drinking establishment to the north side of the street was an attempt at branding itself as high class compared to other saloons. In fact, it was a "gentlemen's club."

The Iris reported when The Oxford Club opened the three-story building it was fitted up in palatial style not sparing expense. The lobby had polished cherry partitions with frosted glass to keep the lobby separated from the bar. The bar-room was large and had every modern convenience. The walls and ceilings were decorated in orange terra-cotta with gold accents. Pictures and elk heads decorated the walls. There was a billiard room and bowling alley in the basement. *The Iris* reported that citizens found real benefit and pleasure in the vigorous exercise. The lunch counter associated with the bowling alley, according to the article, had the most fastidious culinary line.

The establishment was illuminated by thirty incandescent lights and each room had an electric bell. There were rooms to rent for private events and the second floor had, according to the article:

> … *first class rooms, finely furnished, that can be secured at any hour making the place a first-class European style hotel.*

On November 3, 1894, in the area where The Oxford Club ran its standing advertisement, readers were informed that the election returns would be held at the Oxford the evening of November 6th and invited the public to attend.

Then a strange thing happened. In the spot where the Oxford dutifully ran their ads each week, the paper ran a blank spot. Typed on the spot was, *held for the Oxford.* The rest of the year was a very generic ad that just said *The Oxford Club, Colorado City, Colorado* without a picture or address. Then, advertising ceased for The Oxford, and the prime front-page spot for advertisement was taken over by the Hoffman Hotel. The grand Oxford was gone, a casualty of attempting to break the ever-growing barriers between the upstanding businesses on the north side of Colorado Avenue and those lower-class establishments on the south side.

In 1900 The Oxford was listed as a saloon, run by Gus Hogan, located at 524 Colorado Avenue, which means it had re-located to the south side of the street. The even/odd number system changed in Colorado City after it was annexed into Colorado Springs so that the two towns had the same numbering system. By 1902, the Oxford was no longer listed in city directories.

The Templeton Building as it looked after the Oxford was no longer located in the building. (OCCHS Archives)

The Templeton building is one of the locations that has been rumored to have one of the tunnels that once connected various seedier locations in Colorado City. Was the tunnel built when The Oxford Club was at this location? The very pious Templeton, who built the building, would not have wanted tunnels from his building across to the saloon side of Colorado Avenue. Templeton was known as the father of Methodism in Colorado City. When looking through the archives of the Old Colorado City Historical Society's museum for photographs of the building, an interesting group of photos taped together was found. The notation on the photographs said the pictures were taken during the revitalization of old Colorado City in the 1980s. The photos, taken during renovations, show a doorway on the south, street side, of the building, from the basement of the building. Why was there a doorway that could only lead under the street? Was this the old opening to the tunnel that could have been built when the building was renovated for the Oxford?

Bordellos

Life in the West in the early days did not offer profitable employment for women. Women were expected to marry, have children and run a household. Education was not considered of high importance for a lady in the 1800s. If a woman did not marry and did not have family to support her, or if her husband died, the choice for supporting herself would be menial jobs that paid very little. Housework, sewing, cooking meals, taking in lodgers or factory work, were some of the jobs available to women. Even educated women, such as teachers, were paid low wages.

Some women turned to prostitution. If they were business minded and had a little money set aside, they could open a house with other "soiled doves" to entertain the ever-growing number of men coming west to look for gold or work. The girls that worked in the bordellos were often divorced, abandoned, widowed or uneducated and would be desperate for any type of work and a place to live. They too, like the men who came searching for gold, had dreams of making money quickly. If they were lucky, they might find a man to marry or save enough to go into business for themselves. Very few did though; it was a hard life. Often it was their "man" who led them into prostitution.

Although there were the few that did "strike it rich" as in the case of a prostitute known as Red Stockings, who made $100,000 and had a lot of "fun" in Leadville. She owned a stable of horses and wore Paris gowns. So yes, there were some prostitutes that liked the excitement the lifestyle offered.

Colorado City's very successful Madame, Laura Bell McDaniel, had been a married woman with a child when it became necessary for her to support her family. She went into business and ended owning the most successful brothel in Colorado City, a lovely brick house with beautiful lawns. She also provided her mother with a respectable home and one for her daughter as well. Many women who went into prostitution as a business were disowned by their family, Laura was not. She kept her home life and her work life separate, and her family accepted that she was supporting them. Laura's daughter lived at today's 2622 W. Vermijo in Colorado City. Her mother and stepfather John Kistler lived at 310 South 24th Street. Both houses were paid for by Laura.

Laura was known as the Queen of the Tenderloin in Colorado City. All Madams that ran "Sporting Houses" had to pay fines each month to the city for the number of "ladies" that worked for them. Laura's establishment had the most "young ladies" trying to make a living and paid the most fines. Her business was a high-class business and her girls charged up to $250 for one visit. Remember this was when women made $2 a day to do laundry and Laura could make $500 a night at her bordello.

One way to tell the most successful bordellos is by looking in the records at the fines paid. In 1909 from July to November, Laura Bell paid $365 in fines. Also, in Colorado City in the same time period, Bessie Paxton paid $295, Eula Davenport Hames paid $275 and Mamie Majors paid $90.

Laura's establishment, later would become the girl's dorm for a Christian school. Later still it would be converted to a nursing home. (Photo from the People's Bible College used with permission)

Laura will always be a woman of mystery due to her untimely death. In *Brothels, Bordellos and Bad Girls*, Jan MacKell writes when Colorado City voted for prohibition, saloons and prostitutes moved. Laura stayed in Colorado City. Laura listed herself at that time as a landlord who rented furnished rooms. The city authorities wanted her gone. Laura was arrested for purchasing stolen liquor that had been taken from a home in the Broadmoor area near Colorado Springs. Laura was acquitted of the charge.

The day after her acquittal, Laura and her niece were taking a friend, Dusty McCarty, to Denver, reportedly for a doctor's appointment. Her car mysteriously went off the road and rolled. Dusty had been almost totally blind for several years. He had been known for making the best drinks in Colorado City and was a bartender. He was being taken care of by Laura.

The Colorado Springs Gazette reported on January 25, 1918, that a car two hundred feet ahead of Laura's car, driven by Colorado Springs Deputy District Attorney Jack Carruthers, Carl Blackman and George Curtis, saw the accident. They stated Laura Bell's car, which was being driven by her niece Laura Pearson, wobbled then rolled three times. They were one mile south of Castle Rock. Laura and her niece both died from injuries, Dusty survived with minor injuries. The car was only going 30 miles per hour. Some historians wonder if Laura had been run off the road. The *Colorado Springs Evening Telegraph* of January 26, 1918, stated that the accident would remain a mystery as the road was hard, there was no chance of skidding and the car was not driven at excessive speed.

In the 1940s, Laura's sporting house became a temporary dorm for girls when the People's Bible College, a religious school, built a campus in the run-down Red-Light District. Later, Laura's home became a nursing home. One staff member of the nursing home came to the Old Colorado City history center to ask about the history of the building. He had heard it was a bordello. He asked if we could explain why there were blocked up doors that had been closed off in the basement. It is believed that those doors were the beginning of tunnels. *The Time Traveler in Old Colorado*, by Jim Easterbrook, states that Laura's place was part of the tunnel system and her friend Dusty, even though he was blind, could find his way around the tunnels and brought businessmen to Laura's establishment through the tunnels.

The list below, compiled by Sharon Swint and Leo Knudson of the Old Colorado City Historical Society, shows just a few of the Madams that ran bordellos at the height of Old Colorado City's wild days. Washington Avenue is now Cucharras Street. Ladies that worked for the Madams were called boarders in business directories.

- Laura Bell McDaniel, 615 Washington Avenue – This establishment was an all brick building and included three boarders, plus musicians

- Mamie Majors, 617 Washington Avenue – Three borders and two musicians
- Nattie Dayton, 619 Washington Avenue – Two boarders
- Emma Burns, 621 Washington Avenue – Four boarders and a musician
- Annie Wilson, 620 Washington Avenue – Three boarders. This was a "colored" bordello

Many other ladies of the evening such as Anna Boyd, Bessie Paxton and Eula Davenport lived in Colorado City. It was a hard life. For some, like Eula, marriage followed to the son of one of the most successful businessmen in town, none other than the son of Mr. Hames, owner of the Hoffman.

To highlight the evil ways of these women, *The Iris* would refer to articles that appeared in other papers as not good advertising for Colorado City. These articles pointed out the "undesirable citizens" who made the news who lived in Colorado City. In an article in July of 1909 the headline read, "Unprofitable Advertising." It stated the *Evening Telegraph* came out with a story on Annie Wilson, better known as Red Em. Annie had returned to Colorado City to conduct her dive in the Red-Light District. Even though forced to leave the city, she had returned. Selina Moore, another keeper of a dive was arrested for selling liquor without a license.

The Argus also was reporting on the undesirable characters of Colorado City. They reported that Red Clancy was taken to court due to vagrancy. *The Argus,* according to *The Iris,* printed stories like the one below that hurt the reputation of Colorado City:

> *For some time, this city has been overrun with pimps and hangers on. It is conceded that not for many years have so many been around. Red Em was compelled to leave two years ago…she*

was notified by police that she could not 'light' here again, but she says she has as much right as the rest.

The editors of *The Iris* and *The Argus* did not see eye to eye on many issues. The editor of *The Argus* often pointed out the inconsistency between city officials and their treatment of various illegal acts and the inconsistency of the punishment for those illegal acts. *The Argus* felt these issues hurt the city far more than pushing a total "dry" agenda *The Iris* would take. For an example, Nellie McCarthy, keeper of the Brunswick rooming house, was fined for selling liquor without a license. *The Argus* pointed out in an article dated January 14, 1910, saloons were not allowed open on Sunday and rooming houses could not sell liquor, but many brothels got away with it by just paying their fines:

When a saloon keeper pays $1,000 a year license, it is high time that the dives and joint keepers be put out of business. While it is wrong, why should so much fuss be made about a saloon being open on Sunday, contrary to ordinance, when a person can go to the bawdy houses and buy all the intoxicants wanted.

Mamie Majors bordello at 617 West Washington, today Cucharras Avenue. (OCCHS Archives, photograph by Don Kallaus)

City Ordinances
Trying to Rein in Bad Behavior

As citizens put more and more pressure on the city government to rein in the unsavory businesses on the south side of Colorado City, city ordinances were put in place. Colorado City saloon owners became inventive to get around the ordinances. One of the ways to keep away from the prying eyes of judgmental citizens and the law, was to build tunnels. Easy access to unsavory places meant a gentleman could be unseen with easy routes to escape the law.

Most information on tunnels has been through word of mouth or rumors. The Old Colorado City Historical Society confirmed there was a tunnel in the Colorado City Beer Hall as ancestors of Jacob Schmidt have given us family history to that effect. Stories passed down state that Bertha, wife of Jacob, made him brick up the tunnel. Signs of the bricked tunnel have been viewed by the Historical Society.

Other locations of tunnels have been verified by Sharon Swint and Leo Knudson from the Old Colorado City Historical Society. They verified tunnels running from a gentlemen's clothing store to a saloon and tunnels from brothels and a gentlemen's club running to drinking establishments. One of the most interesting locations was verified by dowsers and was reported in the *Gazette Telegraph* of January 29, 1978.

Charles Stockbridge came to Colorado City in the 1870s. Stockbridge, a merchant, owned the largest wholesale wine and liquor business in the state outside of Denver, according to the *Gazette*. When Colorado City was founded in 1859, then became incorporated in 1887, Stockbridge would be the towns first mayor. His residence was on the site of an early hotel in Colorado City. After a New Year's party, the home was destroyed by fire. It was believed the fire could have been started by some of his political enemies. Stockbridge rebuilt his home in brick, which still stands today. It had to be hard to be a politician who owned a brewery in a time when liquor was becoming unpopular. There have been rumors that a tunnel went from his home to the brewery and another tunnel that was a fire escape led to Fountain Creek. The *Gazette* article described what was discovered by the dowsers:

> *Divining devices used by Severson and Kumph agreed there's a tunnel going east from the building, with Krumpf's instruments estimating the tunnel ceiling is 10 feet from the ground surface and 16 feet to the tunnel floor. Severson's instruments estimated it is 9 feet 7 inches to the floor of the passage. They traced the tunnel across 28th street until it teed off with another passageway.*

> *In addition to having indication from their instruments of a tunnel extending from the building in a north-south direction toward Fountain Creek, they also located a narrow (about 30 inches wide) passage from the house to a room under the parking lot. Estimate of the room size is approximately 12 by 15 feet, the ceiling about 10 feet from the surface of the ground and the floor about 17 feet down.*

One of the former residents who lived in the home for many years told the Old Colorado City Historical Society there was a tunnel behind the fireplace on the main floor that led to a hidden room.

Stockbridge home at 28th and Colorado Avenue was said to have a secret room under the mound in the side yard.
(OCCHS Archives, Ellis Collection)

Gambling was against the law, but many saloons allowed gambling. In 1895 the United States banned interstate transportation of gambling materials. This limited the movement of the new slot machine that was invented by Charles Fey of California in the late 1890s. Gambling all but died at the dawn of the 1900s. In 1901 Colorado City's city ordinances outlawed gambling and by 1906 it was illegal in the State of Colorado. By 1909 slot machines were illegal in San Francisco. Nevada passed laws making it illegal to deal or play poker, bridge, whist, fan-tan, faro, craps, slots and horse racing. All gambling was outlawed in Nevada from 1913 till 1931. By 1910 almost all types of gambling were illegal in the United States.

Colorado City monitored its saloons, gambling halls and ladies of the evening through its city ordinances. The city was aware that the ordinances would be broken and fines collected were placed in the city coffers and helped pay for city services. Below are some of the ordinances from the turn of the century for Colorado City. Each had its own fine.

Women were not allowed in a saloon
Drunks could not be served alcohol
Children could not enter a saloon
Saloons must close at midnight and open again at six a.m.
Saloons would be closed on Sunday
People could not be drunk on a public street
Gambling was prohibited
Prostitution was prohibited (Fines were collected monthly)
No singing in a saloon or billiard house
No shooting of guns
No vagrants could be on the street. If you were healthy and could work, you must work. If you have no money to pay the fine for being a vagrant, you must leave Colorado City.

One pending city ordinance was addressed in *The Argus* on June 4, 1909. Credit was given to saloon keepers for their rapid move to accept the ordinance that would require windows and doors not obstruct views into saloons to make it easier for law officials to observe compliance with other ordinances:

Apparently, in anticipation of the adoption of the pending ordinance for the removal of screens from the front of saloons, some keepers have already taken out all blinds, etc. Whether they have taken time by the forelock, remains to be seen, but they have certainly laid hands on the windows and doors obstructions. It is a commendable move, and should be encouraged.

The question of liquor was often a topic of debate and filled *The Iris* with articles. Even Colorado Springs had citizens that did not agree with the growing sentiment against the sale of alcoholic beverages. *The Colorado Springs Gazette* ran an article on January 16, 1909, regarding drug stores in Colorado Springs rumored to sell small quantities of alcohol for medicinal purposes. Headlines read "Liquor Interest Back of the People's Ticket." It reported that:

Faction Wants Clauses Inserted Licensing Clubs and Permitting Sale of Intoxicants in Small Quantities, Which Would Result in Wide Open Town.

Details of the plans of the "blind-pig" druggists of this city, who are boosting the People's charter ticket, in order that their own liquor interest may be advanced, became known yesterday. These druggists hope to have two clauses, highly beneficial to them, inserted in the charter...one clause provides for the sale of liquor in Colorado Springs for "mechanical, medicinal and sacramental purposes," and the other fixes the annual liquor license fee to be paid by the local clubs.

The *Gazette* article pointed out the only difference between a drug store and a saloon would be that the men who drink must stay inside of a saloon, whereas the man whot buys liquor in a drug store may take it elsewhere.

What did the local citizens think of liquor? We do know the Women's Christian Temperance Union held a contest in Colorado City's schools giving a prize for the best essay written on the topic. The results were announced in the newspaper and young Luther McKnight won the contest. Upon his death Luther McKnight, a lover of Colorado City, the town where he grew up, gave the Old Colorado City Historical Society funds to purchase the building where the Society's museum is located. Printed below is his winning essay, which gives insight as to how school children were aware of the question of legal alcohol in the early 1900s. Although not completely accurate, it is fun to read what children thought.

What is the Harm in a Glass of Beer
Luther McKnight

Beer in general is the name of any malt liquor, but as used in the U.S. and on the continent of Europe it means lager beer. In England, beer usually means ale. Beer is usually made from barley, malt and contains 3 to 5% alcohol. Alcohol forms the vital principal in all the spirituous liquors consumed in the world. "What is the Harm in a Glass of Beer?" is a question many people ask. "One glass will harm no one" is answered. But as alcohol is vital in beer, they may as well answer "a little alcohol will harm no one." A little alcohol will create a hunger for more and often for a larger percentage of alcohol in the drink, so stronger beer is used.

Some physicians (?) class beer among tonics and stimulants. Many of note class it among poisons. Beer attacks the kidneys rendering them unfit for their work, thus other organs are overworked and the blood is in bad condition so that in case of accident, blood poison is apt to set in, and in case of sickness, beer drinkers are unpromising patients. Many beer drinkers know the result of drinking and will not take a drink when there is important business on hand. Brewers call beer a temperance drink, but beer leads up to a stronger drink. So, you have another drink. So, it can't be called a temperance drink.

Another reason for wanting people to believe that beer is a temperance drink is because they wish to sell it in places where spirituous liquor must be abandoned. Besides the harm a glass of beer may do to you, another seeing you drink may himself take a glass. Your influence is being used in the wrong way. The expense of beer drinking is to be considered by many. The money thus spent could have been invested as to have given more strength. It is hops that give beer its fragrant flavor. Hops serve to deaden the nerves and used with alcohol acts similar to opium.

Hops soon affect the kidneys and as beer stimulates for a short time, more beer is taken to stimulate the kidneys. When the kidneys are ruined, whiskey is often resorted to and the drinker dies a drunkard. It is well known that the Germans who are great beer drinkers often have kidney trouble. Beer is often doped, that is, things are put into it to create an appetite. Beer is sometimes sold in places where spirituous liquors are not allowed to be sold. Beer contains to 3 to 5% alcohol and therefore is spirituous liquor. Some people say "Beer will not hurt you if you don't drink it."

One night, just after payday, a bunch of foreigners bought a keg of beer. At first, they drank and were merry, later they drank and were drunk. They had a fight over some small thing and were put in jail for drunkenness and disturbing the peace. Of course, they had a trial and were fined a small sum. You never drank that beer but your taxes are high because of the officers of the law that are appointed to track down such disturbances. You have to help keep up the jails and the court houses. Some neighbor of the beer drinkers, although he never drank the beer, had to forfeit his nights rest because of the swearing and fighting. A man may not swear when in his right mind, but will swear when full of beer. When it *becomes known that he swears, he may have a harder time to get a job. Beer sellers argue that taxes will be increased if beer and other similar liquor are not licensed. In some places, this is true. If a man cannot spend his money for beer, he will save several dollars. His tax may be increased a dollar, but he has cleared a few dollars. Beer sellers argue that the taxes of anti-beer drinkers will be raised. Many anti-beer drinkers would be glad to give the extra money to live in a peaceful town. Beer sellers say it will ruin the town to stop the sale of spirituous liquors. They do not agree with the average businessman.*

Many businessmen are working to rid the town of people who are selling spirituous liquors by the people's permission.

The harm in a glass of beer may be simply stated in classes: First – personal harm. The glass of beer creates an appetite for more and stronger beer. The result is often ruined kidneys, which means very bad health and often death. Second – influence. It is hard to refuse a glass a beer when offered by a friend who drinks. You might hurt his feelings. Third – beer drinking is hereditary. If you drink it, it is probable that your children will inherit the appetite. It would be better to leave them the money you spent for beer. Fourth – expense. With some people the expense of drinking must be considered. Some one-glass beer drinkers are in the habit of spending a dime for a good drink once in a while. When they argue that instead of spending the dime for beer, they will buy some popcorn or peanuts. But when the time comes, they buy the beer too. They often become great spenders and sometimes borrow from the government, the bank or rich man and as a result are supported at the states expense for a term of years. Fifth – When you are full (of beer), you disturb the neighbors and other members of your family when they would like to be sleeping. Sixth – You put your city to too much expense hiring police and judges. Seventh

– You give yourself and your family a bad name often making it hard to get a job. A large abdomen does not usually increase a person's opinion of you.

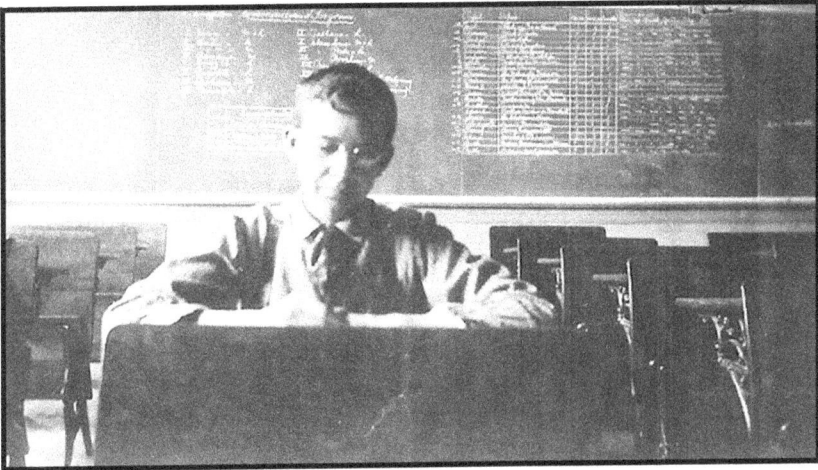

Young Luther McKnight around the time of writing his winning essay on the evils of drinking.
(OCCHS Archives, McKnight Collection)

Colorado City and the Red-Light District - On Fire!

As groups such as the Women's Christian Temperance Union and home improvement societies grew in popularity the fiery battle lines were being drawn between the citizens of Colorado City: those who wanted prohibition and those who did not. At the beginning of the battle looming, local newspapers choose not to run articles regarding saloons, gambling and prostitution. No longer would you find articles in the paper that celebrated new businesses that supported liquor, as they had done when the Hoffman and the Oxford had been built. Only a small notice regarding the death of one of the "lady" workers might appear. Generally, little was written regarding the south side of Colorado Avenue. It was a subject not to be discussed among the moral citizens and was bad publicity for the city. One news item that did bring focus on the lifestyle of those in the Red-Light District was when fires occurred. Often fires could be associated with the Red-Light District.

The end of the 19th to the beginning of the 20th Century was a time of notable fires in the United States; Milwaukee, Chicago, San Francisco and New York all made national news. Building materials, oil lamps, tar roofs and unsafe working conditions were causes of many fires along with conditions in cities that made it difficult to fight fires.

Fire equipment was over twenty minutes away when fire broke out at the Union Oil Company in Milwaukee in the late 1880s. Before the fire was subdued, 27 blocks of warehouses and dwellings, an area of one mile long and one mile wide, were destroyed. Twelve Chicago firemen died at the 1893 World's Fair when a warehouse caught fire. The Windsor Hotel caught fire in 1899 on 5th Avenue, New York. Nine people jumped to their death before the firefighters arrived. Although the fire department arrived just two minutes after the alarm was sent, the construction of the hotel caused what was called a "quick burner." Ninety-two people died in the fire. The Great Seattle Fire of 1889 destroyed 25 blocks, including the entire business district. Only one death was reported. The Great Bakersfield Fire of 1889 destroyed 196 buildings and killed one person. In 1906 the Great San Francisco Earthquake and Fire took 80% of the city and approximately 3,000 lives. Fires of great magnitude would be written about in the local Colorado City newspapers.

Hose Co. Number 1. (OCCHS Archives, Muskwinski Collection)

In the 1890s fire service concerns such as water supply, size of streets, compactness of a city, and the type of material used in building began the conversation on starting national standards for fire-fighting. Colorado City was also concerned with fires and tried to keep the best equipment available for the city as noted in *The Iris* in May of 1898:

> *Fire Marshal Minium has received the new fire harnesses and has them in place over the pole of the fire wagon in the new fire house. The city team is being trained to get under the harness with very good success. Some very creditable hitches and runs have been made.*

Colorado City was no exception to cities with fires. In 1891 the Star Bakery burned and there was a fire in the roundhouse of the Midland Railroad. Colorado City Glass Works was destroyed by fire in 1892 along with Pearce-Jensen Reduction Company and Steward Stucco and Cement Company the same year. In 1894 the Ute Pass Paint Company was destroyed by fire. Local homes would also catch fire with regularity.

The Antlers Hotel burned in 1898 and although in Colorado Springs, the Colorado City Fire Department helped fight the fire. Later, Colorado Springs would return the favor when the Red-Light District of Colorado City burned.

The City Notes section of *The Iris* often contained news of local house fires:

> *A six-room house in Glasstown belonging to J.W. Hatfield was destroyed by fire early Wednesday morning. An unbridged gully hindered the fire department and prevented their getting to the fire in time to put it out.*

The explosion of a gasoline stove about noon Monday slightly burned Mrs. J.C. Johnsen about the hands and head. It also set fire to the building and goods of the J.C. Johnsen Undertaking Company of 9 South Fifth Street.

On Wednesday, July 1, 1903 fire once again hit Colorado City. The fire broke out after midnight and burned four buildings on Colorado Avenue. City Marshal George Birdsall and two others sustained injuries fighting the flames. Electric wires were threatening to give trouble so Birdsall climbed to the roof and cut the wire so the live wire would not fall to the street where bystanders were watching. He sustained a sever shock that threw him from the building. Nearly suffocating from smoke, Birdsall called for help. Charles Pitman and a colored porter rescued him, both sustaining injuries. Birdsall joined the fire department in the late 1800s and convinced the city council to hire him as both Marshal and Fire Chief. Birdsall would later give up the position of Fire Chief but remained Marshal till 1906. Later he would become the Sheriff of El Paso County.

The 1903 fire was believed to be started by coals dropping on the floor from a stove at the back of the Little Gem Saloon. It then burned Lang's cigar store at 520 Colorado Avenue, the All Right restaurant at 518 Colorado Avenue and ended at the White House Saloon. Colorado City Hose No. 1 ran over 1,000 feet of hose.

Colorado City had a close call in 1904. Because of an early discovery of the fire, it was quickly put out. Great concern was noted in the paper as there were a half-dozen framed buildings adjoining each other which would have been burned had the fire gotten a good hold. A fire was discovered under the floor of Nelson's Jewelry Store at 515 Colorado Avenue. The building was frame construction but covered in corrugated iron. The firemen cut a hole in the floor and flooded the crawl space under the building. The wall became so hot between Nelsons and Stephens' Shoe Shop next door that the paint blistered. None of the jewelry was hurt, but firefighters were becoming more and more aware that construction of buildings played a large role in fire containment.

Another close call came in 1905 when fire was discovered in the kitchen of the City Hotel on Seventh and Washington. When the hose was attached, it was found that the water had been turned off and chemicals had to be used to put out the fire. Damage was small and covered by insurance.

Modernizing Colorado City's Fire Department.
(OCCHS Archives,
Peerless Graphics Collection)

1908/1909 Three Disastrous Fires in Colorado City

One of the busiest times for Colorado City firefighters was the last six months of 1908 and the first six months of 1909. In July 1908, in the early morning, Fritsch's Barber Shop at 516½ Colorado Avenue caught fire. The fire department quickly put out the fire that could have been disastrous for the south side of Colorado Avenue. *The Iris* reported that there were wooden structures on both sides of the barber shop which could have easily caught fire. Although the building would have to be torn down due to damage, most of the damage was in the back of the shop and did not destroy the barber chairs or bath tubs, *The Iris* reported. There was no insurance.

The week of December 4th 1908 was a long one for Colorado City firefighters. Mrs. C. S. Morrison's clothing caught on fire due to a gasoline explosion, which also caught her house on fire. Mrs. Morrison extinguished the fire on her clothes by rolling in the snow in her yard. The fire department put out the house fire but great damage to the home occurred. Then a few days later a gas pipe exploded at Kinsman and Wolff real estate office, but was quickly put out. Two days later fire broke out in the rear of the Arcade Club's restaurant and spread to the buildings on either side. Needing more than the Colorado City Fire Department, the Colorado Springs Fire Department came to their aid. A barber shop owned by Hiram Jordan, Kelly's Pool Room, Fritsch's Barber Shop (that previously had been destroyed by fire) and the Arcade Club were destroyed. The flames were brought under control due to brick buildings on each end of the block. The buildings burned were all wooden structures and were torn down. This fire on the 500 block of Colorado Avenue would have a loss of about $40,000. It would be the first of three disastrous fires in a six-week period.

The next fire was a Saturday early morning fire that broke out in the Red-Light District on January 9, 1909. Nine houses were destroyed on the north side of Washington (now Chucharras) Street between 26th and 27th. The fire, according to the paper, spread rapidly due to high winds, with a total estimated loss of $35,000 - $40,000. The fire started at four a.m. Before sunrise over 100 fires started due to sparks.

The Red-Light District fire was fought in zero-degree temperature and many of the firefighters still had stinging eyes from the smoke when the third fire started on January 12, 1909, only two blocks away. Ridenour Livery Stable in the 400 block of Colorado Avenue, along with the warehouse of Beyle Undertaking Company, also in the 400 block, and a one-story frame house on the corner of Washington and Fourth caught fire with a loss of $26,000 in property and forty-three horses.

The horses, that were staying at the Livery on their way to Monte Vista, along with fourteen carriages, were completely destroyed. The fire started in the rear of the stable on Washington Avenue. Hay stored in the building went up like powder. The flames reached the Beyle warehouse and the nearby home, which were gutted quickly. The occupants escaped from the home with little more than their lives. Colorado City Mayor I. A. Foote personally directed the fire-fighting. He kept four of his horses at the stables, fortunately they were in the front building that did not burn.

Almost the entire town came out to watch the fire. This third fire in a short period of time caused much terror to the town according to reports. Mayor Foote and the Chief of Police had to work quickly to have the debris hauled away as the stench of burned horses was almost unbearable.

Mr. and Mrs. Seeley of 405 Washington Avenue would have perished when their house caught fire but people pounded on their door and shouted. The roof fell in as they went out the door.

**Colorado Avenue looking at the stables prior to the fire.
(OCCHS Archives)**

The below recounting of one of the fires, in the area of prostitution, gives a firsthand accounting of fires at the turn of the century: It was reprinted in the Our Heritage section of *The Sun*, February 8, 1976, by Doyle Trent:

> *Colorado City, January, 1909 – While a group of evangelists stood by last night and shouted "Praise the Lord" the Red-Light District of this city was wiped out by fire. Fanned by a strong cold wind, the blaze consumed the entire south half of the block between 6th and 7th streets, facing Washington Avenue.*
>
> *Fire Chief Ivan Brush said the turnout of volunteer firefighters was the largest ever in this region, and it was only "gutsy hard-fought determination," that kept the fire from destroying half the city.*
>
> *What started the fire is a mystery, but strangely it flared up twice. The first alarm came at 11 p.m. from a business*

establishment known as the "Red Light Resort."

Firemen found scantily-clad women battling a blaze at the foot of a stairwell. With modern fire fighting equipment, the firemen were able to contain the blaze within a few minutes.

Brush said several of the firemen stayed around "just in case it flared up again" and they were still there when the second alarm sounded about 4 a.m.

However, the blaze had a head start before it was discovered, and firemen said it "ran with the wind," threatening the entire business district.

When it became apparent the local fire department could not contain the blaze, a call for help went to the Colorado Springs Fire and police department. Brush said he was told that 12 off-duty policemen immediately came to help.

Among the firefighters were Madams Laura Bell, Mamie Majors and Eula Hames. Their girls, dressed in filmy clothing, also braved the cold wind to help in the battle. At the same time, a group of evangelists who were in the city to conduct a revival meeting, stood by, prayed and praised the Lord. Each time a wall collapsed, they shouted "Hallelujah," and said the fire was the Lord's way of destroying evil.

One of the hardest working firefighters was Jack Diamond, gambler, prospector and gunslinger. At one-point Diamond picked up the cool end of a burning board and threw it at the evangelists, scattering them briefly. But they quickly gathered again as Diamond went back to work, batting with his coat at flames that had jumped from one building to the side of another.

The high winds carried burning embers for several blocks, and owners of homes and stores were on the roofs, battling flames with blankets and garden hoses.

The volunteers included many of the city's politicians and administrators. One house was saved by Mrs. Ira Wolf, wife of the police chief.

When fire jumped to the front porch of the house Mrs. Wolf ran up, tore off her coat, and smothered the flames with it.

Brush said he was amazed at the number of volunteers. He recalls previous fires that did as much damage, but did not attract as much help.

Only a month ago, six buildings on the Avenue in the business district were heavily damaged by a fire which broke out in Lacey & Kranze building. And a year ago, on December 4, 1908, a block of wooden buildings in the business were leveled by fire.

Early this morning the madams and their girls were digging in the ruins, trying to find belongings that had not been damaged. They wore sheepskin and cowhide coats donated by men from nearby saloons.

Their faces were streaked with soot and ruined multicolored makeup. Several of the girls had miners' large leather boots on their small feet.

Nine houses "on the line" had been destroyed. Among the mourners were several city officials. They said the fire also wiped out an important source of revenue for the city. As one official put it "Once a month, the madams would line up in police court and pay their fines. It helps the budget."

The loss of the cat houses, he said, is a great loss to the city.

Only four month later, on May 7, 1909, *The Iris* reported some people of the town were upset because John Guretzsky had been given a contract for $10,000 to erect a building on the site of 'The Mansions' in the Red-Light District, where Laura Bell's brothel had burned. This meant that Laura Bell was building a new brothel on the site of her old building. The fires had driven some of the Red-Light District women away, but they were drifting back. *The Iris* stated that better people stood ready to back the council to ensure the Red-Light District would never again be permitted.

Colorado City Fire Department circa 1912
(OCCHS Archives, Peerless Graphics Collection)

When fire occurred in a business, it took jobs away from many. In August of 1907 there was a fire at the Golden Cycle Mill that caused layoffs. Joel Bates lost his job. Because he was out of regular employment, times got hard for the family and in March of 1908, Joel committed suicide.

News on December 24, 1909 put a horrible end to the year that had been so full of fires. Blanch Burton, of 918 Colorado Avenue, was burned to death when a curtain fell and knocked over a lamp, setting her clothing on fire. Blanch, *The Argus* reported, was a recluse of about 50 years old. Although Blanch was a former Madame, *The Argus* felt it was only appropriate to mention the passing of this human being without mentioning her profession.

Colorado City would go from a bucket brigade to a horse and hose system and then finally in 1912 the fire department went motorized with its first fire truck.

A Little Bit of Fireman's Fun

The fire department was not all business. They were well noted for placing elaborate floats in all town parades. They also hosted events in town. In February of 1897 they ran this notice in the local paper:

Hard Times Fire Brigade. On Tuesday evening, February 16th, Colorado City Hose No. 1 will give a hard times ball at Miller hall, for the benefit of the poor of this city. Like the famous ball of Mrs. Bradley Martin in New York last week, the costumes which will be worn have in a measure been designated. No one will be allowed on the floor who is not dressed in a 'hard times' outfit, that is to say that silks, satins or broad cloth will be tabooed. At or about four o'clock on Tuesday afternoon the entire fire department will answer a bogus fire alarm and make a run to an imaginary fire. The entire force will be dressed in hard times garments and make an extensive display.

Crime

Crime committed in Colorado City was often connected to alcohol and prostitution, but not all of it, and not all crime was committed by Colorado City residents. Robbery, murder and assault were often headlined in the paper.

November, 1896:

> Yesterday morning about 9 o'clock Ralph Pendleburg, night clerk of the Almo Hotel, and Harry Richards, brother of Mrs. Fullerton, wife of the proprietor of the Almo, came to Colorado City from Colorado Springs for the purpose of having a "good time." The young men finally drifted into the Arcade Club about noon. Both were under the influence of liquor. While in the Arcade, Richards got in a dispute with Julius Bailer, an employee, over a bet. Bailer let Richards have his way and paid the bet, telling Richards to get out of the house, as he had trouble with him before. A quarrel ensued and Richards fired on Bailer striking him in the forehead just above the right eye. Bailer fell to the floor and breathed his last at 1:30 p.m.

After the shooting Richards tried to escape but was caught in the alley and taken to the city prison and locked up by Marshal Clark. Pendleburg was also arrested and locked up into a separate compartment.

Richards is 21 years old. When interviewed in the city jail, he appeared to be in a hysterical condition. He claimed that he had been shot and that he had no revolver. He begged for cigarettes. Pendleburg refused to be interviewed. The shooting was done with a 12-caliber pistol which Richards threw aside in the alley when attempting to escape.

Julius Bailer came to this city when the Colorado City glass works was open and was a glassblower by trade. He leaves a wife and two children. He was quite an inoffensive man.

May 15, 1908:

Two Greeks attack H.O. Vanocker and J.O. Orr with knives and guns. Last Friday evening H.O. Vanocker and his cousin J.O. Orr were attacked by a couple of Greeks on Fifth Street who used a gun and a knife in a threatening manner. The Greeks had some dispute with Mr. Vanocker on the street and ran home to get the weapons. When they got back the man with the gun shoved the gun in Vanocker's face while the other approached to strike with the knife in the back. To quote Mr. Vanocker "The man is in bed yet." The Greek ran off and threatened others as he ran with his gun. The Greek who used the gun was arrested.

December 21, 1915:

Sheriff George Birdsall returned Wednesday morning from the east having in his custody, Arthur Hamilton, the alleged bank robber, who single handed held up and robbed the Bank of Manitou at noon on the 7th of this month. Hamilton, in a conversation with the sheriff admitted that on the afternoon of the robbery officers were on his track and they were so close to him he could hear them talking, but he was properly armed and it was a good thing they did not come up to him or there might have been something more serious as he would not have been taken without a fight.

When captured in a fashionable hotel in Indianapolis, Hamilton was armed with two automatic revolvers and he was spending money like he had plenty of it.

The one crime that received headlines and was followed in many editions of *The Iris* in 1889 was the sensational robbery of the Midland Depot. The December 19th edition told the following:

The Midland Depot Captured by Highwaymen
A battle between police officers and the robbers
Officers in pursuit
One of the boldest robberies ever executed in this city was successfully carried out at the Midland depot last night. At the time of the robbery three men were in the office... The night train for Cripple Creek had gone through and the station men were waiting for the Gulf Midland from Denver. In the waiting room were four men who were thought to be waiting for the train. Without a moment's warning the door leading to the waiting room was forced open and before the railroad men had time to collect their senses the robbers were in the room and had the men covered with their revolvers. The door to the safe was closed but not locked as Mr. Woods had a short time before selling tickets for the Cripple Creek train. The robbers opened the safe door and finding the cash drawer locked broke it open with a crow bar. As near as can be learned about $60 was secured. They also took

Woods and Christopher's (Midland employees) watches, after which they departed going in the direction of town.

Midland Depot of Colorado City
(OCCHS Archives, Current Collection)

Police were called and soon hot on the trail. When catching up with the culprits, the police were met by a volley of shots. Fourteen shots were exchanged. Although the Colorado Springs police were also called, the thieves got away.

Colorado City residents would follow the news of this robbery and the pursuit of the criminals for a week until they were caught in Pueblo. According to the newspaper, a warrant from Justice Faulkner's court, the editor of *The Iris,* along with the Marshal went to Pueblo to discuss a lead they had received. Two of the criminals got wind the police were closing in and decided to leave town. They robbed the police station of horses and a buggy, but were later apprehended. The other two criminals were arrested in a separate incident. Both stolen watches had been put up for $20 at a Pueblo gambling house after the criminals had blown all the money taken from the Midland playing faro.

As expected though, many crimes were committed that were associated with saloons. The worst location was the Arcade Saloon.

June, 1905:

Jim Lacy, proprietor of the Arcade saloon, another of the places raided by police for keeping open on Sunday, was tried in the district court Tuesday and Wednesday on charges of keeping his saloon open on Sunday, was acquitted.

In an adjoining room, and back of Jordan's cigar store is what is termed the "Pasttime Club", where drinks are dealt out on Sunday. Lacy claimed he sold no liquor on Sunday, but sold it to the club prior to Sunday, which dealt it out to members. It seems that Lacy's bartender and porter work in the Pasttime Club on Sunday, while his brother has charge of the place.

Later developments may show who the proprietor of the Pastime Club really is.

October, 1908:

A sensational event that had set gossip a-going a little out of the ordinary took place Tuesday evening about 10 o'clock. James Lacey, proprietor of the Arcade saloon and his brother in-law, Mike Burke, walked into the saloon of A. Perrine and took the money out of the cash register claiming it was due him on an election bet. While Lacey was attending the cash box, Burke held Perrine at bay with a revolver.

Many times the Arcade Saloon was in the news, although the Crystal Palace was the only saloon that lost its liquor license for being too unlawful. Suicides, breaking liquor codes, robbery and murder did not close the Arcade but The Crystal Palace was too wild for Colorado City.

Another type of criminal establishment located in Colorado City was known as a hop den; a place that served opium. According to *The Argus* of August 23, 1912, one hop den that was a menace and disgrace was none other than the log pioneer cabin known by 1912 as the "old capital building." Multiple raids occurred on the illegal business located there and inhabited by blacks, Chinese and "low whites", according the the paper, but to no avail. They immediately went back into business. The pioneer cabin had served as a territorial meeting place and had once been the office of Dr. Garvin. By 1912, the run-down old building was used as a Chinese laundry. The paper believed:

A bawdy house is not generally considered as bad in a community as a hop den. There is chance for reform for the former, but not from the latter…No decent person frequents such a place.

THE NORTH SIDE

Upstanding Businessmen

Colorado City was founded by businessmen with hopes of creating an important supply town. In those early days it was the entrepreneurs that were the dominant businessmen in the area. Too often historic writings of Colorado City dwell on the saloon keepers and the wild side of town. Colorado City's citizens were so much more: railroad workers, people in the mining industry and a multitude of small businessmen came to the area wanting to be successful. Those businessmen opened grocery stores, outfitters for miners and farmers, lumber mills, flour mills and they speculated in real estate. Although by the late 1890s saloons became the dominate business on the south side of what is today's 2500-2700 block of Colorado Avenue, they employed only a small percentage of people in town. The south side of the 2400 block belonged to small business owners like Anthony Bott, one of our city founders. The north side of Colorado Avenue was the home of banks, department stores and the opera house. For every saloon owner or employee, there were far more family businessmen and women in Colorado City.

Anthony Bott arrived in the Pikes Peak Region in 1858 and was instrumental in the growth of Colorado City, its water system, its cemetery and the securing of the location of the Midland Shops of the railroad. At the time of his death in 1916 the *Gazette* headlines read: *Death Claims Man Who Came to Find Gold and Built and Empire Instead.* Bott would be listed in the *Polk City Directory* as having his real estate office in today's 2400 block.

One early family business in Colorado City was a grocery store. It was originally owned by Judge Stone who moved to Colorado City in 1863-64. Mary Emma Stone, his daughter, became the 1st post mistress and married James Faulkner. J.D. Faulkner would take over the store and become a prominent leader in Colorado City, holding the positions of Mayor and later Justice of the Peace.

The Faulkner Store circa 1893 located at 631 Colorado Avenue, per The Polk Directory (north side of 2600 block today). The Faulkners raised eight children in the home above the store which stayed in the family until 1928. (OCCHS Archives, Tate Family Collection)

The first *Polk City Directory* (*The Directory*) for Colorado Springs, Colorado City and Manitou Springs came out in 1879. Colorado City had a total of 99 listings that first printing. These listings would not reflect if the person listed had a spouse or children connected with their listing. There was only one saloon listed in town at that time owned by Henry Coby. It was located on the north side of Colorado Avenue and West of Second Street .

Although there were places previous to 1879 where alcohol was available, Mr. Coby's was the first saloon that was recorded in *The Directory* in Colorado City. Years later when Mr. Coby passed away in 1912, *The Argus,* in an article in March 11[th,] reported that the pioneer was 79 years old and still living at 715 Colorado Avenue when he died. Coby came to Colorado City in 1858 as one of Colorado's first settlers. His trading post was the site of the meeting of the 1st Colorado Volunteers when they organized during the Civil War. Mr. Coby had been a member of the Third Colorado Cavalry and was one of the survivors of the battle of Sand Creek in 1864, according to the article.

The first directory also shows there was a brewery owned by Mr. Stockbridge and Mr. Elwell that employed three other people. The brewery was located on the south side of Colorado Avenue, but the warehouse was on the north side of Colorado Avenue, in the store that was originally built for the Gehrung family in 1868.

The Directory of 1879 for Colorado City list the city trustees as men with occupations of farmer, livery man, wool grower, miner and general store owners. The city listed two hotels, the St. James located at the north east corner of Colorado Avenue and West First Street and The Hotel, located on the south west corner of Colorado Avenue and West Third Street. Many workers listed these two locations as their residence. There had been previous hotels in Colorado City, but by 1879 these two were the only ones listed. There was one church, the Methodist Episcopal Church with Rev. James Easterly both the pastor of the church and the Principal and Superintendent of the one school in town.

Also listed as citizens of Colorado City were: twenty-eight freighters, eight teamsters, seven miners, four laborers, five ranchers, three farmers, three plaster of Paris mill workers, three mill workers for a mill on Fountain Creek and three workers for a flour mill and seed company. There were two people who worked in the livery trade, two merchants, and one each attorney, gardener, Justice of the Peace, constable, charcoal burner, wool grower, dressmaker, blacksmith, and domestic. There were five women without professions listed. There was one man that listed his occupation as a 'gent.'

Inside the post office found in the Faulkner store.
(OCCHS Archives, Reid Family Collection)

By 1882 the *Polk Directory* listings for Colorado City had dropped to 54, then down to 47 in 1886. The description of Colorado City found in the 1888 directory said there was hope for growth in Colorado City due to the Midland Railroad. The 1888 summary of Colorado City stated the total population (men, women and children) was about 100 in 1886, 400 in 1887 and at the time of printing in 1888, the population was 1500.

Workers for the quarry in Red Rock Canyon
(OCCHS Archives, Reid Family Collection)

In the late 1880s some of the largest employees in Colorado City were the Colorado Stucco, Brick & Cement Works, the Ute Pass Mineral Paint, Colorado City Glass Works, a brewery, a bottle works factory and a quarry. There were only twenty-four people listed as working in a saloon. Then, with the reduction mills, railroad and Cripple Creek traffic, things began to grow in Colorado City, with opportunities for many small businesses. The saloons began to boom but so did honest family businesses. In 1894 businesses were listed under "type" of business and saloons grew to twelve, nine of which were located in today's 2500 – 2700 blocks. Saloons represented only a small percentage of employment for the growing Colorado City.

It is important to understand the number of family businesses that were not associated with the saloon businesses to really understand Colorado City residents. Many families lived above their stores and were raising their children in the downtown area. Mothers of these children would be a significant factor in cleaning up the city. Below is a listing from *The Directory* that shows the number of non-saloon businesses that were in one south side block of Colorado Avenue in the late part of the 1800s. These small businesses were right next door to the saloons and Red-Light district.

From the 1890 *City Directory*, today's 2400 block
408 – Odle & Green, Grocers
410 – H.C. Shimp, Gents Clothing, Reading Room
410 ½ - C.N. Hamlin, Shoemaker 412 - Abe Newman, Dry Goods
414 – C.D. Taylor Dry Goods
416 ½ - Mrs. M.A. Hunt, Groceries
418 - F.J. Brown, Tailor
418 – August Tyroff, Tailor
422 ½ - G. W. Blocksome, Barber
422 – J.K. Vannatta, Attorney at Law
424 – Mrs. Thomas McCabe, Restaurant
428 – James Apted & Co., Commission House

Note the address that was listed for C.N. Hamlin Shoes was list-ed in *The Directory* at one address and in the newspaper at another. Advertising tended to be more accurate than *The Directory*.

The Iris liked to feature successful businessmen in the paper as a way to advertise the city. One article featured Squire Pond, a first-class watchmaker. Pond's business in Colorado City had been so successful that he joined with businessman Henry Ellithorpe, also a watchmaker. Pond and Ellithorpe's jewelry store, located at 412 Colorado Avenue above the post office, became a staple in the city causing *The Iris* to feature the two men as leading business men in 1892. The article noted that the gentlemen were both single and known for being very sociable. Pond and Ellithorpe were recognized for their abilities as the Colorado Midland Railroad appointed them watch inspectors for the Midland Company.

Both Ellithorpe Jewelry and C.D. Taylors Dry Goods and Clothing would relocate on the north side of the 500 block in 1900, but the Taylor family remained living upstairs at 414 ½ Colorado Avenue. Businesses often moved from one location to another as the central business district changed. The 2400 block across from today's Bancroft Park, which held Bancroft School at the time, was always a small business block.

From the 1900 *City Directory*, today's 2400 block
420 ½ - Kinsman Real Estate with a notary
422 ½ - Anthony Bott Real Estate

424 - Star Restaurant

424 ½ - A.H. Weston, Physician

426 - Mrs. Sawyer, Millinery

428 - Ott & Newell, Groceries

428 ¾ - D. Mull, Cigars and Confectionery

428 ½ - Ascough Loan Company

428 ½ - C.L. Cunningham, Notary

Pond & Ellithorpe,
THE JEWELERS.
Next door to the P. O.

If you want anything in the line of
Gold Watches,
If you want anything in the line of
Silver Watches,
If you want
Charms or Badges,
It you want
Pins or Eardrops,
If you want a pair of
Bracelets,
If you want
Native Jewelry,
If you want
Souvenirs,
If you want Watch or Jewelry repairing, or, Jewelry
Manufacturing,
If you want anything usually found in a first-class Jewelery Store you will find it, at a reasonable price, and just as represented, go to

Pond & Ellithorpe,
THE JEWELERS.

Colorado City was very proud of the entrepreneurs that brought business to town. The Templeton Building made front page news when it was complete. *The Iris,* on August 26th, 1891, featured the Grand Opening of the Woodland & Acheson dry goods store in the building, Their motto was, "Eastern Prices and Cash Sales".

Also advertised almost every week for the rest of the year were, "Rooms for Rent" at the Templeton Flats run by Mrs. S.A. Brownell. The newly furnished rooms had new carpet and furniture with baths and water closets on the same floor. One month later advertising began for the Templeton Dining Hall which was billed as a first-class restaurant.

Colorado City was so excited when the Templeton building was completed that on September 19, 1891, *The Iris* ran an article, taking much of the first page of the paper, on the enterprising business people behind the *Best Structure in the City.* The article presented to its readers portraits of both of the businessmen that would occupy the building and the contractor Albert Allen.

South side of today's 2400 block of Colorado Avenue. It was the small business block for Colorado City. (OCCHS Archives) Advertisements shown are from the *Colorado City Iris.*

Albert Allen came to Colorado City in 1887 and with Jacob Stansbrey built the Ash Block and many residences. It was reported the Templeton Building was 50 x 90 feet on the ground and was three stories high. The basement had 8-foot ceilings, the second floor had 12-foot ceilings and the third floor had 14-foot ceilings. There were two staircases, front and back. It took 250,000 bricks and 75,000 feet of native timber. The building was provided with a complete sewerage system. It took three months to erect and complete the building.

The dry goods store that was located on the first floor was owned by Woodland and Acheson. It opened with a $10,000 to $12,000 inventory, containing dress goods, bedding, millinery, ladies' and gentlemen's furnishings, notions, and jewelry.

Mr. Woodland was twenty-eight when the store was opened. He had been in retail business previously in Boston. Woodland was a family man. His partner William Acheson was single and thirty when the store opened. He also came from a retail background.

The second floor of the Templeton building was used for room rental and the top floor was used exclusively for lodge purposes. The forty-five members of the local Masons and ninety members of the local Knights of Pythias orders secured a three-year lease. There was a reception room on the third floor and space for a banquet hall with a kitchen. The lodge room was carpeted and furnished with leather sofas.

North side of Colorado Avenue held multiple businesses in the early 1900s. (OCCHS Archives)

Henry Templeton, an early investor and businessman in Colorado City, hauled equipment by an ox team from the east to erect one of the first flour mills in the city. He worked with stock and traded in real estate. Templeton was known for his strong religious beliefs. He was known as a strict Methodist, and more than likely in favor of prohibition. His obituary stated it was largely through his efforts that the First Methodist Church was built. But, always a businessman, he sold the Templeton Building in 1893 for $20,000. It would then house The Oxford Club.

The Argus also featured new business endeavors in town. When an old dry goods store on 412 Colorado Avenue was turned into a "Modern Bargain Bazaar" by Mr. Bernstein, large crowds were clamoring to shop due to his new business idea. Mr. Bernstein said the store's policy was people could look without buying, return things bought if dissatisfied and Mr. Berstein would even return your streetcar fare for the trouble. This was a new business concept. The store intended to capture the trade of not only Colorado City, but of Colorado Springs, Manitou and the entire vicinity.

The 1890s - Financial Times for a Changing Nation, Changing Colorado City

The nation, including Colorado City, was changing as it approached the end of the 1800s, In the years that followed the discovery of gold in Cripple Creek, the country went through difficult times as it moved from an agricultural nation to an industrial one. Immigrants were coming to the United States wanting employment. Those people who had a vested interest in the growth of Colorado City had a great desire to advertise the advantages of living in the area. Workers were needed and the newspaper ran numerous articles regarding the desirability of Colorado City for families.

As the United States became more industrial, farmers organized several large regional groups that provided social and educational programs for better farming practices and also worked toward political and economic reforms to benefit agricultural communities. These regional interest groups were the beginnings of what was known as the Populist Party. This political party also attracted mine workers. The Populist movement was in support of free coinage of silver, public ownership and operation of transportation and communications facilities, restriction on immigration and a shorter working day.

In the late 1890s railroads engaged in practices that made it hard on family farmer. They charged high prices for hauling freight and even higher prices for freight going a shorter distance. Freights for large shippers were granted rebates. This made it expensive for small farmers to haul goods.

Modernizing farming brought new, but expensive machinery. With the population growing through immigration, the need for more and more food grew. With industrialization in the cities, the number of family farms shrank. Farmers needed the new machinery to compete, but cash was not available. Interest rates on loans were high. Reforms were needed, causing the ideas of Populism to gain support.

As the United States was emerging as an industrial world leader, understanding and anticipating banking and monetary problems of the nation was difficult. From the time of President Washington until 1873, the U.S. had coinage on a bimetal system for legal tender. In 1873 the government stopped making the silver dollar. Miners called this the crime of 1873. Western miners called for free coinage of silver and Western congressmen pushed for and passed legislation such as the Sherman Silver Purchase Act. Passed in 1890, it was to help stabilize the price of silver. It was a constant struggle to keep the economy sound and the dollar strong. The question of a gold standard or a bimetal standard was hotly debated. The United States had experienced economic growth in the 1870s and 1880s, but in the 1890s came hard economic times.

In the election for Governor in 1892, Colorado elected Populist candidate Davis Waite; both Democrats and Republicans lost because they did not back the free coinage of silver. In 1893, President Cleveland convinced Congress to repeal the Sherman Silver Purchase Act which he felt was responsible for the economic crisis.

Colorado and the United States were hit hard with the decline in the dollar. Banks failed, railroads went bankrupt, and unemployment soared. It became known as The Panic of 1893. In Denver and throughout Colorado, the topic on most people mind was the continuing Denver Depression. Almost every Colorado resident had a vested interest in the success of the mining industry. The repeal of the Sherman Silver Purchase Act caused prices of silver to fall and the prices fell even further due to an overabundance of the metal. Mining companies cut wages; many people were without work. This news would be extensively covered in the local papers.

The economic depression in the United States caused unrest in many parts of the nation: New York City had 12,000 tailors strike against working conditions; Pullman Company workers went on strike. President Cleveland did not bring back prosperity as hoped. The lack of prosperity hurt the first Democratic President since the Civil War and left room for a Republican victory in 1896. Shown on campaign posters was William McKinley running on the slogan of "prosperity."

In February of 1894 *The Iris* ran, in multiple editions of the paper, articles on Colorado City and the advantages of living and working in the city. The articles read like news, but seemed more like advertising, building hope for the future. News of Colorado City would travel east, bringing more people and investment to the area. The future looked good with the growth of gold production in Cripple Creek.

One article gave insight into Colorado City:

Colorado City is one of the newest as well as the oldest towns in the great and growing state of Colorado. All have heard how the town went to sleep, Van Winkle like, and slumbered for many years, but many have not heard how she awoke with the building of the Colorado Midland railway and of her progress of wealth and population since that time.

The article went on to expound on the location of the town between the residential City of Colorado Springs and Manitou, the Saratoga of the West. The three cities were connected with Colorado Springs Rapid Transit street railroad as well as connected by the Rio Grande and Colorado Midland. Colorado City, the article boasted, had three great industrial plants and a monthly payroll of $60,000. Its population was 3,000 and the city was practically free from debt. Real estate was better priced in Colorado City than in the two surrounding cities with business lots going between $900 and $2,000.

Other articles pointed out the clay from city founder Anthony Bott's land used in pottery and brick manufacturing, the glass works and the local paint factory along with the local stone quarries. Other advantages of living in Colorado City were the shops at the Colorado Midland Railroad; the roundhouse with fourteen stalls, the machine shop and a mill for making lumber. Another industry mentioned in *The Iris* was the Steward Cement and Stucco Works.

The local paper was the biggest supporter and advertiser for Colorado City during the trying times of the early 1890s. Not only did the paper focus on an industrial growth time for Colorado City, but also focused on family life in the area and the social scene. *The Iris* pointed out one aspect of Colorado City life:

The number of churches and secret societies of Colorado City is not behind the average town either in the East or West.

The article continued its praise of Colorado City stating there were five congregations that had church buildings within the city limits. The Methodist being the oldest, the Church of the Good Shepherd (Episcopal), the Catholics and Lutherans both had nice buildings and the Baptist, with their new church building recently completed.

Also reported in *The Iris*:

It would be hard for a new comer who is a lodge man to be lonesome in our midst.

The newspaper reported that the school enrollment was growing each year and local students studied Latin, algebra, geometry, rhetoric, English and music, as part of their curriculum. There were twelve teachers in 1894 and the Colorado City strived to hire only the best. The school library had 300 volumes. Also noted in the article:

The pride of Colorado City is her public schools and that her citizens take so much interest in their children. Parents from eastern homes often express wonder at the excellence of our schools.

It is no surprise that as word circulated on the employment opportunities and wonderful family environment, many new families moved to the area.

Respectable Women

The 1890s were interesting times for women. Although still the "fairer sex" who loved fashion for both their manner of dress and for their homes, the rights of women and the suffrage movement were also becoming priorities. Reading the local newspapers of the time you can get an idea of things that interested women of Colorado City.

Women 1900s. (OCCHS Archives, Ellis Collection)

Local News and Gossip

The local news was always important and the paper had a section for just that purpose. *The Iris* in the 1890s had a section containing local announcements; who was born, who died, who was sick and with what horrible diseases, who was going to travel, who came to visit the area, who moved, who was fixing their house, who got married, who was throwing parties and who was in trouble. These announcements, like the ones below, kept readers informed and entertained:

> *The YPCE of the First Baptist Church will be giving an entertainment that is a laughable farce called 'The Precious Pickle'. Cost is only 25 cents.*

> *Spiritualism, Miss Grace Andrews and Henry Crindle will hold one of their wonderful séances in the light at the Red Men's hall this Saturday evening. All manifestations are under strict test conditions. Admission is 50 cents.*

> *The Gentile Club is giving a sheet and pillow case dance next Thursday night.*

The mumps, pneumonia, dyspeptic problems, rheumatism, diphtheria and mountain fever were but a few of the sicknesses attributed to Colorado City residents during the 1890s. Mountain fever was a term used by Mountain Men for any fever obtained in high altitude. In the 1800s the term was commonly used by people for any unexplained fever. The whole town would know people's ailments as they were announced in the paper along with advertisements that would cure everything:

> *Stacey Pennel is at work again after a narrow escape from an attack of mountain fever. Miss Park, teacher in our city schools,*

is still confined to her room with mountain fever. There is little, if any, change for the better.

Health and happiness are relative conditions; at any rate, there can be little happiness without health. To give the body its full measure of strength and energy, the blood should be kept pure and vigorous by the use of Ayer's Sarsaparilla.

Most coughs may be cured in a few hours or at any rate in a few days by the use of Ayer's Cherry Pectoral.

Lottie Smith of the 5th grade, Bancroft building, was run down by a bicycle while going to school on Thursday and quite badly hurt. She received several cuts about the head and her body was severely bruised. Superintendent Lawrence of the Midland was riding the wheel and sustained slight injuries from the collision.

**Three Colorado City women were ready for their outing.
(OCCHS Archives, Dunn Collection)**

Some announcements in the paper were a bit of juicy gossip:

> *A young girl known as Bessie Howard, an inmate of a sporting house, tried to leave the world by the morphine route Tuesday night. Dr. Smith and Attorney Watt were summoned and administered ipecac in large doses. The girl survived and the voyage across the dark river for a while was postponed. Another, Belle Bake the Colorado City cyptian who took morphine was buried from Fairley's undertaking room yesterday – Her companions at Colorado City paid the cost of the burial and did not spare their money in doing it in good style.*

Unfortunately, the definition of cyptian could not be found, but the lady took morphine and that was not good. It is to be assumed that both of these women were from the Red-Light District and often the only thing printed about the "ladies" was a good piece of gossip that pointed out the evils and follies of an unacceptable lifestyle.

Fashion

There were many sections in the paper for women in the 1890s that dealt with the fashions of the day and rules of etiquette. An article entitled "Fashion Fluttering" appeared in *The Iris*:

> *Bows, knots and loops, perched on long hair pins and of all shades are coquettish and feminine for young ladies. The neatest and most refined looking bathing suits worn this season are made of black jersey with cap and stockings en suite.*

Popular was the color rose pink as it went well with black. A suggested hair style was a low braided chignon, with hair waved on the sides and drawn down over the top of the ears. A Parisian revival of an old and not so becoming fashion was noted in the paper:

Sleeves are larger and fuller because the look in Paris is broad across the shoulders.

One article in *The Iris* noted that women needed to pay closer attention to hair that shows on the back of their head, when going to the theatre. Others will stare the entire evening if:

Symmetry is lost or straying locks, straight and stringy, fall over the collar.

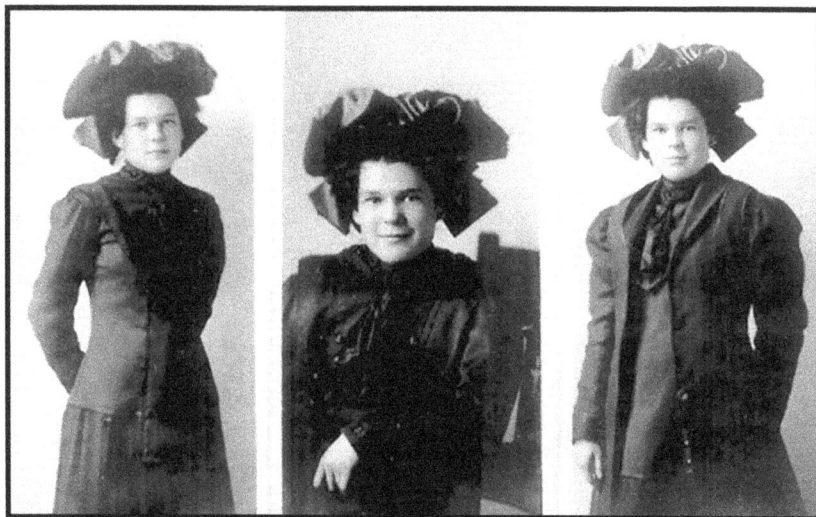

**The perfect suit and ribbons on the hat.
(From the OCCHS Archives, Dunn Collection)**

The Argus also carried an article about fashion at the theater. On June 17, 1910 it was reported that theater managers were upset and wished ladies to remove their very large hats as those who sit behind

behind were not laughing. The new "monitor of Hampton Roads" fashion of styling hair that was as high as a hat was also an obstruction.

The blazer suit was a very significant fashion for women according to one writer. Nearly every woman on the street would have a suit with a bell-shaped skirt, a light shirt waist top covered by a blazer of the same fabric of the skirt. Blue was the fashionable color, and suits should be made of good serviceable material suitable for all weather. This style of suit was appropriate for all age of women:

> There is much agitation regarding the unhealthy dress of women. There is a theory among some, however, that when women are properly educated on their needs, they will quietly evolve a comfortable and sensible mode of dress, and quietly adopt it.

One article in *The Iris* informed Colorado City women that home pillows filled with pine or fern leaves should be placed on divans. Rose leaf pillows were also fashionable, but almost impossible to obtain as rose leaves were hard to collect. The paper reported the difficulty of gathering sweet lavender, noting that:

> The summer girl among her other preparations for the coming season is packing away a dozen or more bags filled with sweet lavender for the home.

In the Etiquette Section was an article written by a man regarding women and their parasols. He noted how to properly carry parasols so that they actually cover the sun from the face, noting that women thought it fashionable to carry parasols differently. Parasols were made to keep ladies from the sun. Too many girls carry them upright when the sun is coming from an angle, he stated. The writer continued with regard to parasols:

94

Did you ever notice what irresponsible creatures they are, these dainty-bits of feminine loveliness, when the summer weapon was placed in their hands to work havoc in crowds. Tearing off bonnets, knocking aside hats and just grazing the sight of many a person who are made nervous by their threat. A cow with a musket would be as harmless as a new day-old baby in comparison with the holder of this feminine bit of warfare.

In the newspaper was an article on the importance of a chaperone for American girls receiving calls from gentlemen at their home. Even when family approved of the gentleman, parents should lay down the law before liberties have been secured the article suggested. A young woman will condemn herself in the eyes of the public if seen to be alone with a young man. Many parts in the West allow this to be done with smiling consent of good society, but in Eastern cities, it is considered a violation of the code of good form.

The writer concluded that if men were allowed to be with young ladies alone, many may look back upon this social evolution with regret.

Another article talked about "Playing Gooseberry." A gooseberry was the term given to the third person that walks along with or is a chaperone for a young lady and her beau. The practice of asking a girlfriend to take a walk with a given young lady so that she can meet up and walk with her beau in an appropriate way was not fair to the third party, forced to play gooseberry, according to the newspaper.

Suffrage Movement

The Woman's Christian Temperance Union founded in 1876, had a very active chapter in Colorado City. Many women of the W.T.C.U were also involved in the fight for women's suffrage. As a result, because they were a strong lobby for anti-liquor, some men feared woman's right to vote, as they might use it to prohibit the sale of liquor. Finally, in 1919

U.S. Congress voted in favor of the 19th Amendment which was ratified in 1920 giving women the right to vote.

Prior to 1920, in 1893, a referendum on suffrage was held in Colorado to ratify a proposed constitutional amendment prohibiting discrimination against women voting. When it passed, it was the first time in U.S. history that a state referendum passed suffrage for women. The following year three Colorado women were elected to the Colorado House of Representatives. Just prior to that vote an article appeared in *The Iris* entitled "Tallmadge on Woman's Rights." The article was a reprint from the *Ladies Home Journal*. The opinion of the author was that if woman wanted the right to vote, she should have it, just as if man wanted to keep house, he ought to be able to keep house, stating:

There are masculine women and there are effeminate men.

The reporter's theory was we have no right to interfere with anyone who is doing anything that is righteous and questioned:

Do we legislate how a brown thrush should fly or a trout should plunge?

Although that seemed very forward thinking for the day, the writer continued with the following:

I know there are women of most undesirable nature who wander up and down the county, having no homes of their own, or forsaking their own homes, talking about their rights. We know very well that they are fit neither to vote nor to keep house. Their mission seems to be to humiliate the two sexes with no thought of what any one of us might become. No one would want to live under the laws that such women would enact, or to have cast upon society the children that such women would raise. The best rights that women can own she already has in her possession. Her position in this time is one of congratulations.

What did women have that they should be congratulated about? They had the God given right to make a happy home according to the article. Although the article started very positive regarding women's right to vote, it continued on to say woman's best right is given not by legislature, but by the "Grace of God", the right to make home happy:

She should make it the most attractive place on earth; it is the only calm harbor of the world. Even if your home is humble, you can, with your faith in God and your cheerfulness of demeanor, gild it with splendors. H.O.M.E. What right does woman want that is grander than to be the queen of such a realm? iInsignificant seems all the words of voting.

This article seemed to believe women had the right to vote, but it surely tried to make the right seem insignificant. It also went on to warn women readers that they should be careful in wanting to enter the area of the society of men:

Women should make sure the atmosphere they enter is pure and clean and that women might be more conspicuous by their absence than their presence.

When Colorado women received their right to vote, many Colorado women would help with the nation's right to vote. The 1890s must have been an exciting and challenging time for women!

Colorado City Soldiers and Cuban Independence

The 1890s were a time when the United Kingdom, France, Germany and Japan were dramatically expanding their overseas empire holdings in Africa, Asia and the Pacific. The public opinion in America held little desire for the United States to have a colonial empire, although Cuba did attract American attention.

Cuba and Puerto Rico in the West Indies were the last remnants of Spain's former empire in the Americas. Revolts occurred in Cuba against Spanish rule. Propaganda against Spain was being published by newspapers owned by Joseph Pulitzer and William Randolph Hearst which called for war to support Cuban Independence. Although the business community lobbied against going to war, they did want to safeguard United State's investments in Cuba.

With newspapers pushing their support for the Cuban revolt against Spanish rule, many Americans began to draw parallels between the American Revolution and the Cuban revolt against their colonial oppressors. Republican President McKinley supported peaceful negotiations with Spain, with the U.S. part of the negotiations. When Spain recalled the Spanish Governor from Cuba, the U.S. Counsel in Cuba sent a request to the U.S. State Department to send a U.S.

warship to Cuba to ensure safety of U.S. citizens if any revolt took place. While the United States Ship (U.S.S.) Maine was docked in Havana an explosion sank the ship. Most Americans believed the cause of the explosion was unknown; 250 of the 355 sailors died, causing Congress to appropriate $50 million for defense. To this day there have been reports that claim the explosion was internal to the ship and others that say it was externally caused by a mine.

Today we talk about "False News" and are familiar with the saying "History Repeats Itself." This also occurred during the 1890s. To sell more papers publishers Hearst and Pulitzer alleged Spain was to blame for the sinking of the U.S.S. Maine and exaggerated accounts on how Cubans were being treated by Spain. Articles were embellished to cause emotional responses from readers. These national news items would be reprinted in smaller papers throughout the country. With the sinking of the U.S.S. Maine, Americans demanded action. Congress considered a joint resolution for support of Cuban independence. Colorado's Republican Senator Henry Teller proposed the Teller Amendment to ensure the U.S. would not establish control over Cuba if a war occurred. An ultimatum was sent to Spain to withdraw and give Cuba independence. In April of 1898 the United States began a blockade of Cuba and Spain declared war on the U.S.

The war with Spain was the top subject locally in *The Iris* and names and places like Dewey, Roosevelt, the Rough Riders, Cuba, the Philippines and Guam would be discussed locally. The residents of Colorado City would read the following headlines:

1st Battle with Spaniards which Results in Victory for Rough Riders and Regulars
Taking of Ft. San Juan – Spanish Fought Like Demons
Clothes for Soldiers – The Making of 150,000 Uniforms
Our Soldiers Suffer – Terrific Rains in Santiago

When the call came out for volunteers, notices such as the following showed up in the Local section of *The Iris*:

Abram V. Worley, of this city, was accepted as a recruit for the First Colorado Volunteers Thursday. He will go to San Francisco in time to join the third Manila expedition.

Another notice stated:

Seven young men quit work at the Midland shops this morning and will enlist for the war with Spain.

Percy Dunn, from Colorado City, joined the 7th regiment, Company B, which was stationed at Santiago de Cuba. He wrote a letter to his friend C.F. Birdsall of Colorado City which was published in *The Iris*. He had left with the troops in July for Cuba. They marched to Santiago where the Americans forced the Spanish into the city and had them surrounded. The country, he reported, was one big battlefield for miles around Santiago. He did not think the war would last much longer. He said that you could not call the Spaniards cowards, even though they were losing, as they *fight like dogs and hit the mark whenever it is in sight, they surprised our men when it came to shooting*. He mentioned Frank Reckendoff from Colorado City was his tent mate. He and Frank enlisted but he heard other Colorado City boys who joined the volunteers went to Manila. He said Cuba was beautiful but there was rain six or seven days out of the week.

Percy Dunn would stay in Santiago and see the Spanish fall and "Old Glory" fly. He would return to the States due to typhoid fever he caught while in Cuba. He would then come back to Colorado City.

Percy Dunn in 1898.
(OCCHS Archives,
Dunn Collection)

Bernard Smith of Colorado City served with the 1st Regimental band at Manila Bay. He wrote to his father that the Colorado Regiment landed in Manila and he was detailed to guard band instruments. He was at sea for thirty-five days straight and some of the men were sick from tropical fever. One of the drummers died along the trip and was buried at sea with military honors. He said heat had a lot to do with the sickness. He wrote he had seen Admiral Dewey and also had seen the remnants of the Spanish fleet that still stuck up above the water. He wrote his dad: *We have remembered the Maine.* Bernard told his dad he was safe as the band did not even have weapons. He said Manila was beautiful and tobacco grew like grass.

One headline that appeared in *The Iris* made the locals with family members fighting in the war hopeful. It reported in its headline: "Wounded in Action – Fatalities of the Battlefield Reduced One-Half. Fewer Amputations Required." The article compared the ratio between the number of men shot who survived during the American Civil War, still remembered personally by many, to the ratio of those who were shot and would survive in the ongoing Spanish-American War. The article went on to describe the great advances in surgery in the years following the Civil War. During the Civil War nine out of ten wounded would die from infection from the wound. During the Spanish-American War, it was estimated about four in ten would die. This did not help those at home when they also heard how many were suffering and dying from yellow fever during their time in the service.

Colorado City would join together to honor men who served the country in previous wars and the current war. *The Iris* posted the following:

> *All old soldiers, both blue and gray, are earnestly requested to meet at B.F. Irvin's store Sunday morning at 10:30 and march in a body to the Methodist Church where Rev. Powell will preach a memorial sermon.*
>
> *Great Demonstration at the shops this morning in honor of Rear Admiral Dewey, the Hero of Manila.*

The largest flag in the Rocky Mountain Region was displayed at the ceremony held in May of 1898. The flag was 13 x 25 feet and had to be custom made. All of El Paso County was invited.

In May headlines read: "Colorado Boys Have Gone." It was reported that amid cheers and tears the first regiment of infantry, Colorado Volunteers, left for San Francisco in route to the Philippine islands. Baskets of chicken and champagne loaded the seats of the train. People greeted the train at every stop in the State to give them a hearty farewell.

Those in Colorado would be proud to read the headline: "Colorado Boys Led – Stormed the Trenches at Manila." The Article reported the following:

The First Colorado Volunteers stormed the outer trenches and drove the Spaniards into the second line of defenses. Then the American troops swept on, driving all the Spaniards into the inner fortifications, where the Spanish commander, seeing that further resistance was useless, hoisted the white flag and surrendered.

Local businessmen used the war to promote their business, some in positive ways such as the Colorado Midland that sold round trip tickets to Denver, to hear war hero Dewey speak, for a one way to Denver price. The May clothier in Colorado Springs had ads requesting "Wanted – 10,000 Recruits" and went on to say some were for Cuba, some for Chickamauga but a majority to shop at the May. In Colorado City, Taylor's Department Store offered the "War with Spain" sale, where they offered their entire store at wholesale costs.

Patriotic sentiments, at a height during the war, prompted Colorado City to declare:

We would celebrate the Fourth of July, and we would do it right.

Months before the celebration a standard notice ran in the Local section of *The Iris,* advertising Colorado City's celebration would feature a grand barbecue of roast beef, mutton, potatoes, pickles, bread and butter prepared for 5,000 people. There would be a parade, speakers, music, contests and toast. All of El Paso County was invited.

Posting of those citizens and businesses that donated to the 4th of July Celebration appeared in the paper. Saloon owners such as N.B. Hames and Jacob Schmidt joined along with city founder Anthony Bott, politician Stockbridge, real estate family the Quimbys, along with many of the store owners in town such as the Taylors Store, Otts grocery, Ellithorpe's jewelry and more. The whole town united for this celebration.

The celebration was reported in the July 9th, 1898 edition of *The Iris*. Outside visitors estimated the crowd at 10,000 but *The Iris* believed the crowd to be about six to seven thousand:

> *The crowd was as patriotic as it was large, and a more orderly multitude never got together. There was no limit to the noise, but the demonstration came from the heart.*

Fire crackers and giant powder fired salutes came from the top of the hill on Lincoln Avenue. A parade at ten o'clock featured floats from each of the departments of the Midland shops. The fire department decorated its fine team and wagon. Another feature in the parade was a float that was a model of the battleship Maine. It was greatly applauded. The procession was headed by Marshal Allen and followed by a platoon of police, the Midland band and a bicycle brigade. Another feature was a cart filled with lemonade. The tank held 750 gallons of lemonade which was served free all-day long.

The celebration continued at a big pavilion where prayer was given, "The Star-Spangled Banner" was sung to remember the brave boys who sang it before fighting in Santiago. The Declaration of Independence was rendered from memory, without notes. One guest speaker ended his lecture:

> *Where the American flag is once raised there will it remain forever.*

The lecture was met with prolonged cheers. Mr. Waycott led the audience in singing "My Country Tis of Thee" and positive news of the war was reported. The crowd rose to their feet, raised hats, cried tears of joy and cheered. Prayer was offered again and the barbecue began. Sports were held on Colorado Avenue opposite the Bancroft School.

In August of 1898 front page headlines ran a proclamation from

President William McKinley announcing to the citizens of the United States that Spain had formally agreed upon the terms for the establishment of peace between the two countries. Hostilities were suspended.

Colorado City would still be remembering the U.S.S. Maine that was destroyed in 1898. *The Argus* printed a chronological story of the battle ship U.S.S. Maine on March 24, 1912. Readers were reminded that she was buried in 3,600 feet of blue water, nine miles off the Cuban shore.

Turn of the Century
Fusion Politics, Strikes, Midland Band, and Local Levity

As the Spanish-American War was ending, a new war close to Colorado City was continuing:

> *What's the matter with these McKinley republicans: are they getting so frightfully numerous that the silver people are all afraid to stray from each other for fear, like the Spanish fleet, they get knocked out one by one? The Wolcott boys are greatly distressing the fusionist least they Deweyize them rights in their supposed stronghold this fall.*

Fusion Politics

This notice was taken out in the local section of *The Iris*. The political war was in full swing, using terms that were fresh on the minds of all after the Spanish-American War.

The late 1890s saw a surge in men turning out to cast their ballots with much political competition for their vote. New party organizations formed and old ones went into factions led by cross party "fusion" agreements or coalitions. A fusion was a joining of different political parties (Populist, Democrats or Republican) for a common goal. In Colorado it was silver.

A ticket of those running under a common goal would be presented after conventions. The upcoming political election would be a heated one with fights at conventions in Colorado.

One of the most violent conventions occurred in Colorado Springs and would be front-page news in Colorado City and in *The New York Times*. Some Silver Republicans were deciding whether or not to join together (fuse) for a single ticket with Democrats and Populists. Those who wanted to fuse were called the Fusionist. Other Silver Republicans did not want fusion. The two sides of the issue were to meet in Colorado Springs at the same time. The faction favoring fusion took over occupation of the Colorado Springs Opera House where the anti-fusionist Silver Republicans had rented to meet the next day. An attack occurred at four in the morning in a struggle for possession of the hall led by the anti-fusion wing who rightfully had rented the spot for their meeting. Shots were fired, killing one man and wounding three others. The papers ran sensational headlines that would inflame the public:

Charles Harris, of Denver, Executed on the Altar by Ambitious Fusionists. Arrival of the Sheriff and Chief of Police Prevents a Wholesale Killing

The article explained the fight had been in progress for some time between the fusion and anti-fusion factions of the Silver Republican Party. The fusionists were in possession of the opera house and placed armed guards in the building to resist an expected attack. The building was opened with a sledge hammer. Shots were fired. It was those holding the building inside that had a number of revolvers and rifles. The Denver papers reported the building had been shot up from the outside, but the local *Gazette* and *The Iris* reported there were no marks from shots on the outside of the building. The anti-fusionist did have the right to be in the building as they did rent it, but *The Iris* did not think that justified them attacking the opera house. It was also noted the fusionist did not have the right to deprive the other side from the building they had rented. It was unknown who fired the shots that killed Charles Harris. It was even said Harris could have been shot by his own, in order to stir up sentiment in their favor; sacrificed on the altar. The fusionists were known to have men who resorted to violence in the past. In 1898 the fusion ticket swept Colorado.

What was the division and fight about? In 1896 the Republicans won an easy victory because the Democrats were divided on the issue of the gold standard versus free silver and the Democrats had failed to restore prosperity. When President McKinley took office in 1897, Congress made gold the standard of monetary value. What was the platform that made the Fusionist win elections in 1898 in Colorado? They wanted the restoration of silver to an equal plane and power with gold as monetary metal. They felt the gold standard that was introduced had proved disastrous internationally. By depriving silver of its rights and vastly adding to the demand for gold, nations using silver had been broken. To enforce the gold standard throughout the world the fusionists felt was impossible. Senator Henry Teller was the leader of the fusionist Silver Republicans against McKinley's Gold Standard Republicans. For Colorado, Teller seemed to be the answer. McKinley would be re-elected in 1900 and serve until 1901 when he died in office. Vice President Theodore Roosevelt would take over the office of President.

Governor Waite to Governor Peabody
Two Sides of Strikes

During the time when Populism was on the rise, Colorado voters in 1892 chose Populist candidates because the economy was based on mining and many of the policies of the Populist movement were beneficial to unions. When Davis Waite was the Governor, he was supportive of mining unions and the workers. When problems led to violence in Cripple Creek in 1893, Waite sent troops to protect strikers. As the powers of the Populist faded, the Republican business wing regained power in Colorado and voters choose James Peabody as Governor. Peabody believed the best thing for Colorado was attracting capital investment; strikes by unions would make Colorado seem unstable. He believed in the rights of property owners and would side with mill and mine owners in strikes.

Life for laborers in the early 1900s consisted of hard work, low wages and long hours. One thing the labor forces relied on was the ability to strike for better conditions. Colorado City was the home of the reduction mills that processed Cripple Creek gold. In 1903, unions submitted proposals for pay increases and better working conditions at the three mills in Colorado City. The Portland Mining Company and the Telluride Reduction company said they would consider the demands; the United States Reduction and Refining Company (Standard Mill) refused to read the proposal. The union struck at the Standard Mill. The mill owners asked for protection from the Sheriff's department and the Sheriff complied. The Governor sided with the mill's management, local residents and Colorado City officials were sympathetic with the union. The Governor approved of sending troops, while local law enforcement said they could take care of any troubles. Troops were sent to Colorado City.

Workers knew there were many immigrants moving to Colorado that would gladly step into their jobs. One thing they did have on their side was the support of the miners in Cripple Creek. If Cripple Creek joined the strike there would be no ore to process. The business leaders in the Cripple Creek district pushed for compromise. Leaders throughout the State became nervous and on March 9, 1903, the legislature passed a resolution calling for arbitration.

After the meeting, the Portland and Telluride management and the union reached an agreement including an eight-hour day, no discrimination, reinstatement of strikers and a pledge for future discussion of wages. Both mills became fully unionized. Management at the Standard Mill would not discuss wages, so the strike continued at the Standard Mill.

After threatened lawsuits by the union against the Sheriff and the officers of the National Guard, the troops withdrew from town on March 19th. Once again Colorado City was under the control of locally elected officials.

The Standard's management and the union could not agree. Not wanting Cripple Creek miners to join the strike, Mayor Nelson Franklin of Victor led a delegation to Colorado City urging the manager of the Standard to compromise. This compromise would lead to a temporary truce.

By August there was still no settlement. The failure to settle the Colorado City strike led to the bloody Cripple Creek labor wars of 1903 and 1904. Eventually the union lost. When violence broke out in Cripple Creek, the Governor declared martial law, sent in troops, removed local officials, jailed union members, and broke the union.

Midland Band and Local Levity

Local news also made front page headlines and made Colorado City extremely proud:

> *The Midland Band, the Pride of Colorado City, again wins First Prize at the Denver Festival of Mountains and Plains – Victory.*

Local bands in towns were at the height of popularity at the turn of the century. Musical performances were one of the favorite forms of entertainment with large numbers of people turning out at local venues and parks to hear their hometown band. Competition between towns and company bands were followed like sports events are followed today. It was reported that tens of thousands of people attended the Denver Festival of Mountains and Plains band contest which lasted three days. It was reported in *The Iris*:

> *Upon the announcement that the Colorado Midland Indian Band had been judged the best of the bands which participated in the contest, spectators fairly went wild with delight and those who stood nearest to Drum Major Billy Bosworth declared that he swelled up several degrees with additional pride. 'Little Willie' takes more pride in the band than does an Indian in his personal appearance when he is on dress parade.*

Colorado Midland Band in Indian costume.
(OCCHS Archives, Reid Family Collection)

First place prize was $300 at the festival. An unexpected floral arrangement was presented by the Second Regiment Band of Hutchinson, Kansas to the Midland Band as a congratulation acknowledgment. Known to be strong rivals, the presentation dispelled the idea of any animosity between the bands.

Ending the year of 1898 with a little levity, one item placed in the local section of *The Iris* in July of that year was as follows:

Four months ago, a young lady of this town unfortunately swallowed a needle and last week one of the doctors took that needle out of a certain young man's right arm. Positively no names will be given.

Colorado Midland Band.
(OCCHS Archives, family scrapbook, unknown donor)

Local police faced many unusual problems along with the day-to-day policing in the city. Colorado City Marshal Allen had to contend with calls to duty. The paper noted the arrest of W.W. Brown for stealing lanterns from the street car track. When Brown was locked in jail, he proved he was insane:

He took off his clothes, smeared himself with coal soot from the stove and made things lively until Marshal Allen took him to Colorado Springs. Mr. Brown thought he owned all the rich mines in Cripple Creek and threatened the officers with all kinds of punishment.

Colorado City's lively boulevard near Camp Creek was an interesting spot to visit for three months. The Ute Indians camped for the summer and as the winter approached departed for Indian Territory the papers reported.

As the century turned for Colorado City, according to the local paper, people attended church, concerts and balls. Births and marriages were announced along with deadlines for dog licenses, excursions offered by the D&RG to fish in nearby Palmer Lake, funerals and the occasional ice cream socials.

In the Good Old Summer Time

Whsn spring was at its end and the good old summer time was in full swing it was time for fun in Colorado City. In the late 1800s and early 1900s there was plenty to do. As America prospered there was more time for leisure.

Lawn party in Colorado City.
(OCCHS Archives, Ellis Collection)

Camping in Colorado 1900. (OCCHS Archives, Muskwinski Collection)

With the end of school, children put on their annual school exhibits. School was opened to display the students work done at school or at home under teachers' instructions. Not just reading, writing and arithmetic, though: basketry, bead work, iron work, clay modeling, burnt word work, carving and cabinet work were some that were featured according to *The Iris*. Also popular were demonstrations on cooking, mending, sewing and weaving along with collections such as minerals and specimens.

In April was Arbor Day. Today we have Earth Day and few participate or know what it represents. Not the case in Colorado City. Arbor Day was a day set aside to thank God for nature and to be grateful for America. *The Iris* reported that each year the day was celebrated in Colorado City in grand style and in 1892:

Every loyal citizen of Colorado City turned out yesterday to witness the Arbor Day exercises at the Bancroft school grounds. From the time the children marched to the grounds till the superintendent dismissed the audience, there was no lack of interest.

The program began with prayer, then the singing of "My Native Land." An essay on the American flag was well received. Poems were read entitled "The Flag of Our Country", "Our Flag" and "E Pluribus Unum." Three girls recited "The Red, White and Blue" followed by a recitation "Forest Song." Then Colorado City resident Michael Murphy read his essay entitled "Our Forest."

Practical jokes filled the air along with spring flowers, Limburger cheese and hot days. On the front page of *The Iris* was an article titled "His New Hat Needed Embalming." The article told the following story:

A good man of Colorado City purchased a new hat and then went for a beer with his friends. When he was not looking, one of the meanest men that lived in Old Town went to the bartender, asked for a thin slice of Limburger cheese and slipped it under the sweat-leather of the hat.

The man returned to work and felt sick, even thought he was dying, but it was the hat that was dead. When he went home the man next to him on the street car moved away. One asked if he had been in Chicago. When he got home his wife figured out what had happened. He tried to bribe the bartender to tell him who had put the cheese in his hat. He was so angry that Police Chief Birdsall had to keep an eye on him. *The Iris* ended the article:

We may get killed for giving away this story, but it is too good to keep, we must tell this one.

Summer was the time for church fairs and the newspaper printed one idea for a fund-raising event, a bazaar with wares to sell representing the different days of the week for women's work based on a mid-19th century nursery rhyme. There would be six booths. The Monday booth would sell everything for washing clothes. The Tuesday booth would sell all things needed for ironing. Wednesday was for cleaning the house and the booth would sell cleaning supplies. The Thursday booth would sell things for sewing and Friday's booth would sell those things for going to the market. Saturday's booth would be the general refreshment booth, as women cooked every day. There wouldn't be a Sunday booth, as it was the day of rest. It could be wondered how this fund-raiser would be accepted today.

Summer outing in the mountains.
(OCCHS Archives, Ellis Collection)

There was an athletic exhibition at the Waycott Opera House in 1904. The event had wand drills, club swinging, and parallel bar work, tumbling, and pyramids. The event was to create interest in exercise and entertain the locals. It was a time when interest in physical fitness was on the rise. Bicycles were a common way to travel for both men and women. Colorado City had a top of the line bicycle shop.

The Iris warned readers that summer was the season of fortune tellers who took advantage. When a gypsy tent blew down with a gust of wind, the inhabitants were upset, but not as upset as the people who owned the property where the gypsies had camped without permission. *The Argus* gave the warning to beware of peddlers who travel to the area in the summer. They suggested to keep your door locked so peddlers won't force their way into the house. It was better to buy goods from local merchants than to shop for things sight unseen and hope for future delivery.

The Fourth of July celebration in Colorado City was one of the biggest summer events. In 1896, five thousand people attended the celebration. Appearing at the festivities was Uncle Sam bearing the flag of freedom. He was escorted through the streets in a parade that was over a mile long. Local businesses and homes were decorated outside with the Stars and Stripes and thousands of yards of bunting. Young boys tossed fire crackers throughout the day.

The day started with canon shot and ringing of church bells. The parade went down Colorado Avenue and Lincoln Avenue and ended at a pavilion west of town. The Midland Band marched with twenty-two pieces. Colorado City Hose Company pulled its decorated cart. The Goddess of Liberty was surrounded by bright young misses representing the original thirteen colonies. Manitou's drum corps followed the goddess. The gold and silver floats came next. Another float representing young America was packed with enthusiastic, healthy, lusty boys who waved the flag. The Woods Free Library also had a float. At a pavilion the Declaration of Independence was read followed by other orators. There was music and dinner, followed by more music.

Concerts in the park, vaudeville and plays, flower excursions on the Midland, trips to Garden of the Gods and Seven Falls, camping, picnics and ice cream socials were all part of the good old summer time in Colorado City.

**Burro ride through Garden of the Gods
(OCCHS Archives, Dunn Collection)**

Men, Women, Travel and Literature – 1900s

In 1893 a referendum ratified a proposed constitutional amendment to prohibit discrimination against women voting in Colorado. This was first time in U.S. history that a state referendum passed women's suffrage into law. For women times were changing. Still, there was a fine line noted in the newspapers of the day between being an independent lady and still keeping femininity. No longer were ladies in the strict, confining, fussy Victorian era, women were heading into the newer freedoms of England's Edwardian times. Although, Colorado City was in America, and the West, Edward VII was the leader of style, art and fashion in continental Europe. Colorado City women looked to the newspaper to follow the trends of fashion. They looked to each other to follow their dreams of more freedoms.

Looking at portions of the paper that were directed at women could be found the following headlines:

Woman's Realm, Making an Ideal Home – The main thing is to avoid over-furnishing.

Purely Feminine – Health and Beauty – Largely dependent on a daily bath...A daily bath should be part of the moral law of every class of society.

Woman's Realm, Makes for Health – Let the meal hour be a pleasant one...gloom and disagreement should be banished, good cheer is an action free of dyspepsia.

In Vogue – Must be Smart to be Attractive – Good looks will not overcome bad taste or carelessness in costuming, style has usurped place of beauty.

It had to be a confusing time for women. On one hand articles came out about the necessity for women to get an education, while another article would warn about men who thought college-bred women were masculine.

On the front page of the July 2, 1909 *Iris* an article titled "Fifty Out of Ten Thousand Girls" reported *Woman's Home Companion* stated out of every ten thousand girls who enter primary schools, only fifty go to college. The rest would become wage earners and home makers and were entirely neglected. Three things the article pointed out happen with an education. First, education offered a sure escape from domestic work, which was of all work, the most menial. Second, when a woman acquired an income, she became more independent. Third, the simplest method of acquiring income was to seek work in the commercial and industrial world. The problem for women, according to the article, was when women work, they become victims of sex competition. They pay a price. Men who work the same job as women found that men's salaries were lowered because women were willing to work for lower wages. While they are equal at work, the male resented the female *interference with his earning capacity and his future.* She would no longer be a matrimonial possibility, which becomes another problem for women according to the article.

Today we talk about a wage gap, it is believed that women get paid less and men get paid more for the same job. The opposite was felt a hundred years ago. It was felt because women would accept less money, when both men and women were working the same job, it would be only economic business practice for the owner of the business to pay the lesser wage to both parties to be more cost effective.

Four turn of the century Colorado City women having a little fun showing off their hair buns and improper for the day, their bums. (OCCHS Archives, Dunn Collection)

Men too were going through a time of mixed messages. New moral values for society were defining a true man as one that didn't drink or associate with those who did. Instead of following the normal behavior of men at the time, drinking and enjoying women, the newspaper carried articles such as the one on January 29, 1909 in *The Iris* titled "Needed Men, Real Men." A call went out for men of strength of character to stand by principal. Men must overcome the evils that continually sap the foundation of social structure. Basically, real men don't drink or misbehave. Interestingly, today's society is still trying to change men. Although time is always changing, some things don't change.

In male and female relationships, one article in *The Iris* reported, under the headline "The First Year of Marriage," problems that occur because men and women are different. Men, the article pointed out, worked all day and need quiet and calm when they got home:

> *They don't want to talk or be talked to. He doesn't want to have to force himself to smile or to think, and least of all does he want to forsake his slippers.*

Women, according to *The New York Weekly*, were shut up all day in the house doing dull domestic duties. When night arrives, women feel a need for change. They want to put on a pretty dress and go to the theatre or call on friends.

One thing that brought the two sexes together in the 1900s was the popularity of travel, seeing the nation and beyond. Tourist travel to Colorado was growing and the papers wrote of the heavy business expected from people traveling by train. In turn, advertisements appeared regularly in the paper by the different railroad lines for Colorado City residents to enjoy seeing new places. Ads appeared in each edition of the paper:

Midland Route – Daily Tourist Cars, Dining Cars and the Finest Scenery in the World

The Rio Grande - $25 to San Francisco, Los Angeles, San Diego, Portland, Tacoma, Seattle and many more - Pullman Tourist Cars Phantom Canyon Line of the Florence and Cripple Creek Railway – Wonderful, Colossal, Subline, Most Magnificent of Colorado Canyons

Shortline – One Day Trip of Wonders – Continuous panorama of nature's scenic wonders

Colorado City followed the travel trends with events like one featured in the paper called "A Trip Around the World." In July of 1909 a tour of people's homes allowed one to find out about different countries: India, Japan, Germany and the United States. Refreshments from the country were served at each home that featured a location. The Colorado City Baptist Church allowed a way for locals to view the world by presenting a slide show of the Passion Play that was held in Germany in 1900.

If you were not able to travel, the paper offered the ability to travel through literature. *The Iris* featured books. Each edition of the paper contained a continued story, chapter by chapter, of a highlighted book. The section would start with a synopsis of the story, and each paper would allow the reader to follow the continuing story. In 1909, for example, the two books featured were *The Loves of the Lady Arabella* by Molly Elliot Seawell and *The Wizard of Oz* by Frank L. Baum. Seawell was the niece of President John Tyler and raised by being *turned loose in a library of good books* at home. She traveled to England, France, Europe and Russia. Readers got a taste of these places through her books. L. Frank Baum was famous among American children with his series of 14 books in the Oz series which let one travel beyond the earth and to other lands.

Today we are surprised when people post everything about their lives on Facebook or the Internet, yet couples of Colorado City had their moves looked at closely too, as the local news printed small tidbits of gossip on local couples. If you travelled, were sick, had gall stones or marital problems, in a small town, it could be printed in the paper. One example from South Side Notes of Colorado City in *The Iris* is found below:

Oliver Casson who gained some notoriety last fall by making a bonfire of his clothing, and house hold goods, including a new $75 sewing machine, at his home, came back last Tuesday, re-courted his wife and together they left on Wednesday for California. Great are the mysteries of the feminine heart! Mrs. Casson is an excellent woman, whose life has been made miserable by a man who the most charitable believe to be insane, yet on his return from six months hiding to escape arrest, one kind word was sufficient to induce her to try life again with him.

Midland Flower Tour. (OCCHS Archives, Reid Collection)

A Picture Says a Thousand Words and a Whopper

The Picture

The following picture is of the 1911 graduating class of Colorado City High School. It was donated to the Old Colorado City Historical Society by the family of Ila Brown. The picture was on a postcard, a very popular way of sending news to family and friends at the time. The graduates are children of businessmen mentioned in *The Iris* and the city directories. Families of Colorado City's past are much like families today.

Ila wrote on the back of the card the names of her classmates. The beautiful handwriting taught at the time was hard to decipher. Luckily, in 1911, if you were a high school student you were listed in the *Polk Directory*.

The Iris featured many articles regarding the city's school students. This graduating class put on the annual senior class play called "A Night Off." It was held at Mack's hall under the direction of high school Principal Louise Sloelzing. The four-act comedy featured all ten of the graduates,including Ila who lived at 317 Monroe Street in Colorado City. Ila's dad George was a switchman for the Colorado Midland.

Martha Kinsman was listed as a student living at 220 S. South Cascade. Her parents worked at the County Jail, Clement as a guard and Jennie as a matron. Cascade Avenue was in Colorado Springs, not Colorado City, but Martha went to school in Colorado City. Don Ellis, a Colorado City historian, reported that Clement Kinsman, Martha's father, previously lived at 114 Colorado Avenue in 1899. Sometime after 1911 he moved back to Colorado City where he sold real estate for several years. In 1924 he sold 320 acres of what is now Bear Creek Canyon Park to Colorado Springs for $11.50 per acre.

Opal Lisenby lived at 409 Olive with her parents Charles and Lottie. Her father was listed as a teamster.

Charlene Sherman lived at 103 Lincoln with parents Mary and Charles and a third party named Morton Sherman. It could be possible that

Morton was a brother of Charlene that was out of school, or a brother to her father Charles. Morton and Mary were listed as working at Sherman & Sherman. This company was listed as a Real Estate, Loans and Insurance firm located at 21 Colorado Avenue. Charles, the father, was listed as the manager of Colorado City Transfer Coal and Storage.

Milton Taylor lived at 429 Lincoln Avenue. His parents were Charles D. and Della Taylor who owned Taylors, a shop for men's furnishings, dry goods, shoes and notions store. The store was located at 500 – 502 Colorado Avenue.

Mark Foote and his family lived at 418 Colorado Avenue. His father Ira was President and Manager of Progressive Stone Foundry Company. Her mother Retta was listed as working in general merchandise at I.A. Foote and Company, a general store on Colorado Avenue. The family lived above the store. Also living at the same address was Donald Foote, an electrician, and Floy, a student.

Otto Foersteman lived at 15 South 4th Street. His parents were Adolph and Henrietta. They are listed both as business and residents of this address but no profession was given. Also listed as living at this address was Julius Foersteman, a bartender for Jacob Schmidt. Otto's sister Matilda, a student, also lived at the home.

Earl Shackelford lived at 122 Lincoln with his father Owen and mother Eunice. They were grocers at 412 Colorado Avenue, right next to the Foote general store. Grocery markets were on almost every other block. The *Polk Directory* listed eighteen on Colorado Avenue starting from 118 Colorado Avenue to 1847 Colorado Avenue in 1911. There were grocery stores, bakeries and meat markets. Shackelford's, according to advertisements in *The Iris,* offered fruit, vegetables, cider, coffee, and tea. They offered a premium plan which enabled you to get many useful and handsome articles in glass, china, granite and tin ware, free of charge, with purchases at their store.

Jim Faulkner lived at 631 Colorado Avenue. This was also listed as a business and residence. James D., Jim's father was a Justice of the Peace & Notary Public. Jim's mother was Mary. Also listed at the same address was Thelma, a student, and Miss Nellie Faulkner, who was listed as the assistant post master of Colorado City. The post office was listed at 419 Colorado Avenue. That would have been across the street from the Foote general store.

Florence Hemenway lived at 315 North 4th Street. Her father William worked as an engineer on the Colorado Midland. Her mother was Muriel.

These ten students that made up the graduating class of 1911 link today with the community that long ago lived on the west side. The students all lived near each other and their families had jobs all close to each other.

The Whopper

One of Colorado City's long-time businessmen was Jack Gillespie. Jack married into the pioneer Nye family, marrying Mayme Elizabeth Nye. The family lived in the Bear Creek Canyon area. Mayme had two sons from a previous marriage, but Jack was happy to take on the boys and give them a stable family life.

Jack was a barber with a shop on Colorado Avenue. As in most barber shops, it can be imagined that a tall tale or two was told by both Jack and his customers. In the October 13, 1911 issue of *The Argus* a story was told, in good fun, about Jack. Local interest stories help in understanding the community living in Colorado City. Apparently, Jack had killed a wild animal near his home in Bear Creek Canyon:

As Jack is too modest to give out his feats, a friend of his came to the Argus and asked that we publish the story just as it happened.

Because Jack lived in Bear Creek, he often saw wild animals. At the time, the paper noted, he had seen a twenty-three-pronged buck in his yard and got his rifle and ran out of the house. The buck was several hundred yards away but Jack, knowing how well he shot, took the shot. The story continues and becomes even more of a whopper:

The Palace Barber Shop, shown in the picture, was located at 516 Colorado Avenue around 1900. The proprietor as J.R. Gillespie. (OCCHS Archives, Muskwinski Collection)

Jack knew his shot had not failed him. Going to the spot he found his prey in a resigned position, the main artery having been severed three feet from the head. Jack shouldered it and carried it home, it weighed 496 pounds…The buck was left hanging in a tree in the yard when Jack saw a huge mountain lion gnawing at its neck, Jack went to the wood pile and picked up a ten-pound broad axe which he had made from ties from the Rio Grande and Midland railroad.

Jack then hurled the axe at the lion, four hundred yards away. By mathematical calculations he arrived at the speed and angle he must throw the axe to hit the lion between the eyes.

The story concluded with Jack killing the mountain lion. As a way to feature local people, the paper published this tall tale of Mr. Gillespie, stating that Jack had been in the area so long that he came when Pikes Peak was a spouting volcano. It was fun to read the story about Jack Gillespie as his family still lives in the area and have donated many photographs and historic items to the Old Colorado City Historical Society. Human interest stories found in old newspapers give us insight into the lives of people of the past.

Gillespie's at Garden of the Gods, (OCCHS Archives, Muskwinski Collection)

World News and World War I

The first permanent and successful transatlantic cable crossed the Atlantic in 1866. Telegraph wires had been carrying news messages for almost twenty years by that time. For the average American, newspapers were still the source of news. Colorado City residents were no different.

Major news stories, both national and international, found their way into Colorado City newspapers. Wars, disasters, major events and new inventions were covered. There was always political news to follow.

Theodore Roosevelt's name often appeared in the news. To be part in the successful Spanish-American War, Roosevelt had given up his position as Assistant Secretary of the Navy to form a volunteer cavalry regiment made of polo players and cowboys. Known as the Rough Riders, the regiment distinguished themselves at San Juan Hill.

Roosevelt disliked political bosses and believed every American should have a "square deal." As a Republican, he would serve as President from 1901 until 1909. Roosevelt believed that big business had grown stronger than the government elected by the people. The Sherman Antitrust Act was put in place to monitor the power of big business, but it was not being enforced according to Roosevelt.

Roosevelt was also in the news for his conservation efforts, pure food and drug acts and monitoring fair rate practices of the railways.

The April 19, 1912, papers carried news of a disaster at sea, the loss of the Titanic. Although no one from Colorado City was on board, Denver's own Margaret Brown had lived through the disaster. The town felt the loss of the Titanic deeply. Newspapers reported the number of lives lost and those that were saved. Articles also appeared on who or what was to blame.

News of the country's desire to build the Panama Canal was of interest and covered in the Colorado City papers. It had long been the desire of businessmen in the United States to build a canal that connected the Atlantic to the Pacific Oceans, shortening the miles and eliminating the need to sail around South America. The need was not only for the financial benefit, but for defense of the country. The project to build a canal had first been tried by the French, but was unsuccessful for financial reasons and tropical diseases. France sold the property rights to the United States for the canal zone in Panama. Panama was part of Columbia at the time and Congress authorized the President to purchase the rights, as long as Columbia agreed. When Colombia did not agree to the terms, the people of Panama revolted and declared independence from Columbia. Panama wanted the economic boom that would occur if the United States built the canal and worried that the United States would relocate the project elsewhere. The United States backed the revolt, sending warships to prevent the military of Columbia from entering Panama.

The papers carried news of the canal project and the difficulties caused by malaria and yellow fever. The army corps of engineers were successful in building the forty-mile canal which opened for traffic in 1914. After the completion, news of the celebration of this event was carried in *The Iris:*

The World's Great Nations Join with American in Celebrating the Opening of the Panama Canal in a Conclave Unsurpassed in History.

This wonderful celebration would culminate with an exposition with exhibits from all the lands showing the world's best inventions and progress. The International Exposition was to be built in San Francisco and set to open in February of 1915. President Wilson would open the exposition, and Colorado City newspapers were filled with stories of the event, even though it would be shadowed by other events that were occurring in Europe.

The July 3, 1914 edition of *The Iris* carried the story of the assassination of Archduke Franz Ferdinand, heir presumptive to the Austro-Hungarian throne and his wife Sophie that occurred on June 28, 1914. This was a time when the great European powers competed with each other for world trade and the sources of raw materials. Ultimately, the assassination would be the beginning step of a war that would reach around the world pitting opposing alliances against one another. England, France and Russia had formed the Triple Entente and German, Austria-Hungary and Italy had formed the Triple Alliance. Europe was divided.

War was always an issue to be reported. On January 19, 1912 *The Argus* featured an article on the cost of battles. It stated that in 1911, lives lost around the world in battles amounted to 72,000 compared to 13,000 in 1910. The cost of war would be remembered when war broke out in Europe in 1914. *The Iris* would carry headlines that read:

Emperor and Kaiser Cheered when Plans are Announced for Massing War Forces

Russia to Aid Serbs

Austria Shells Serbian Capital

President Woodrow Wilson vowed neutrality while running for his second term as President on the Democratic ticket with the slogan "He kept us out of war." News would be extensive following the events in Europe. Editorials would follow containing information on the sinking of the Lusitania:

> *Last week the largest passenger carrying boat in the world was sent to the bottom of the ocean just off the coast of Ireland by a German submarine. Something like two hundred Americans were on board...Germany has announced that waters around England are a war zone. England has done about the same with regard to Germany. No sensible American would attempt to pass the English blockade of Germany. No sensible American should attempt to pass the German blockade of England.*

Colorado City residents would learn terms such as international law, neutrality, national preparedness and getting "calamity fat," or rich from the spoils of war. Prior to the war, the United States was having hard economic times as Europe undercut the price of U.S. manufactured goods. With war, the U.S. economy was on the rebound. Readers of *The Iris* would learn of a new types of warfare, being "shelled from the sky."

Colorado City would follow the news of a world that was divided. The United States would enter the war April 6, 1917. Later that month, the division in Colorado City would end when the town voted to be annexed into Colorado Springs.

THE DIVISION

Clubs, Churches and Secret Societies

Belonging to a social club, secret society or church was one of the ways for people to meet like kind people at the turn of the century. These were the social networks of the day.

When a town was founded in the West, the first things that would appear would be a place to get supplies, to sleep, eat, and a place to drink, followed by a place to be safe and gather. As more families came to an area, churches or a meeting hall were of great importance. If the town grew, schools and a library would soon follow. For those frontier towns that were truly successful, an opera house would be built. Also needed was a newspaper to tie the town together, a link with the outside world. Colorado City had them all.

While saloons and gambling thrived on the south side of Colorado Avenue, the north side of the street contained Colorado City's growing need for family entertainment. Opera houses were the center of art, culture and entertainment. One hundred and fifty buildings called opera houses were built in Colorado between 1860 and 1920. Most no longer exist. Many burnt down as gas lights of the time caused fires. The Grand Opera House in Cripple Creek and the Grand Opera House in Pueblo both met that fate. Today only one third of the buildings that held opera houses remain. Only a very few are still used for opera. The Tabor Grand Opera House in Denver became a parking lot. Central City has the oldest surviving opera house in Colorado.

The building that held Colorado City's opera house, the Waycott, stands today. Over the life of Colorado City, the building held opera, vaudeville, plays, theatre and lectures. One handbill advertised a "Carnival of Commerce Extravaganza" held at the Waycott Opera House in 1906. Sponsored by the Ladies' Town Improvement Society, part of the proceeds went to the Society's work.

Why look at churches, organizations and clubs that people joined? They held great influence on the values of communities. Looking at the people who attended them and the growing desire for environmental and personal improvement, can be seen the downfall of liquor's acceptability.

Women wanted a voice in improving society through the opportunity of education, careers and, heaven forbid, the right to vote. Women wanted not only to improve their lot in life, but that of the cities in which they lived. The period after Queen Victoria's death and before WWI would see a rise in the Suffragette movement.

In 1874 the Women's Christian Temperance Union was organized. The W.C.T.U. would be one of the most influential women's groups of the 19th century. They had an office in Colorado City and their work cut out for them. It was the W.C.T.U. that pushed for saloons to be closed at midnight in Colorado City, instead of being open 24 hours a day. They pushed for saloons to be closed on Sunday. Monthly meetings and events sponsored by the W.C.T.U. were greatly attended by the women of Colorado City. In May of 1909 their posted meeting in *The Iris* was a review of the book *The Great American Frauds*. The review stated the book covered the percentage of alcohol contained in many of the proprietary medicines. It also explained many medicines, cough drops and headache powders contained cocaine or some form of opiates that should be as feared as death itself.

Although a city ordinance would be passed to close saloons on

Sunday, drinking did not stop. On the Sunday following an April vote in 1909 that was an unsuccessful attempt for prohibition in Colorado City, *The Iris* reported the following:

> *The large number of drunks arrested last Sunday created not a little wonder as to the sudden outbreak. The Iris very seldom refers to the police court business because we do not consider the constant mention of this evidence of the work of the saloon as tending to give Colorado City the fair name abroad, she so much covets. But when 13 drunks are run in on a single Sunday, the day when the saloons are supposed to be closed and no drinks sold with which to make drunks, one cannot be blamed if he begins to look about for the cause of it. Coming as it does, on the first Sunday after an election to which the saloon's succeeded in carrying the town wet, it looks bad to say the least. Either the outgoing police suddenly became lax in watching to enforce the Sunday closing or some saloon men were inclined to celebrate their victory by prying the lid off in spite of police and ordinances.*

December 23rd was Crusade Day for the W.C.T.U. and nearly 150 calendars were distributed in 1909 with sayings that supported their cause. Popcorn and candy were also distributed to promote the cause. A Christmas tree was decorated at the W.C.T.U. Hall and all Colorado City children were invited to a party. In January was Old Folks Day and there was another social event. The W.C.T.U. together with the Loyal Temperance Legions held free lectures. There were very few newspapers at the time that did not report on an event of the W.C.T.U.

Improvement societies were another step toward refinement and generally making the community beautiful. Village improvement societies had their development in small town America in the late 1800s. They were part of a rural reform movement. Colorado City was no exception. Reading the local papers shows Colorado City's Town Improvement Society was very active; holding banquets, talks and events to raise money for the town parks and to clean filth from the town. They pushed for law enforcement and for the city council to clean alleys and yards that were eyesores.

The Improvement Society held events in town for all to participate. Contest were held to vote for the house that kept the best yard with prizes offered to children of Colorado City who grew the best vegetables and flowers. The Improvement Society held contests for babies; not for beauty, but for weight. Colorado City wanted good, fat, healthy babies. Each year when the Improvement Society had its flower show, names of those who contributed were printed in *The Iris*. Having your name in the paper must have been motivation to support the event!

One of many examples of the Improvement Society's activities occurred in 1908 when a large campaign was held to place a pavilion in Bott Park. Anthony Bott was one of the city founders and still living at the time. *The Iris* reported on the fund raising event:

> *The women started out on Colorado Avenue to learn how the business men of the city feel in regard to a pavilion in Bott Park. At three o'clock the days skirmish was over with the following casualties.*

The casualties were those who's names appeared in the paper as contributors. Topping the list was Anthony Bott, followed by saloon owner N. B. Hames. Both men gave almost five times as much as other businessmen. Other saloon owners such as Jacob Schmidt gave to the town Improvement Society's cause along with most of the family run businesses in town.

Men became civically active. Secret societies, lodges and clubs were of most importance. Belonging to a society or club gave social standing and a mission. One active club in Colorado City was the Improved Order of the Red Men. Those who belonged had to be white, male, believe in a Creator and able to support themselves. The origins went back to the Boston Tea Party. Club members stood against the government spending money unwisely. Originally women were not allowed to join, but in 1885 a women's branch, the Daughters of Pocahontas, was established.

The Oddfellows also met in Colorado City. Their organization was based on the principle that people need to elevate themselves and society through humble service. They believed in treating all people with dignity, pursuing truth and adhering to equality, justice and righteousness. Members had to know the difference between right and wrong and believe in God.

Also, in Colorado City, were the Knights of Pythias. They were a fraternal order and secret society formed in 1864 on the belief of loyalty and friendship. A member must be at least 18 years of age, not a professional gambler or involved with illegal drugs or alcohol, and believe in a Supreme Being. They believed in providing for "worthy Pythians in distress" and helped victims of national disasters and the underprivileged.

The Brothers of American Yeomen and Modern Woodmen of America were fraternal orders that helped hard working men insure themselves. They promoted healthy jobs in healthy states. Saloon keepers need not apply.

Although many of the secret societies, churches and organizations had lofty goals, (promoting good health, a Christian life, responsible government, elevating society and taking care of the poor) some of their purpose was giving residents ways to socialize. Throughout the year, all of these organizations held sponsored events, and along with the local theatre, Colorado City was an entertaining place to live. Newspapers were filled with invitations to attend events and articles about events. Below are just a few mentioned in the local papers in a short period:

Old Fiddlers Contest Success in Every Way: Given by the Pythian Sisters was a success in every aspect. The attendance was large and nearly $25 cleared for the lodge...As a grand finale the banquet hall was cleared and an old-fashioned country dance was participated in.

The Boiler Maker's Ball: Monday nights was a social and financial success. The attendance was large, the music splendid and the dancing continued until two o'clock.

An Indian Social: Prof. Al Jenson has generously consented to deliver his noted lecture on "the Ancient Red Men of the American Continent; their habits, customs and peculiarities." After the lecture the usual athletic entertainment will follow.

Idle Hour Theatre: Packed to capacity every night this week, owing to the high-class vaudeville acts put on by the Lovelys, which will continue till Saturday night.

Big Shows Coming Soon: Cole & Rogers Railroad Shows in all their magnificent splendor will exhibit at Colorado City June 27 and two performances will be given rain or shine, under two mammoth waterproof tents.

St. Patrick's Ball: to be given in Mack's opera house by the Pythian lodge of this city.
Lecture-Entertainment Course: Baptist Church announces its people of Colorado courses for the winter months...The list

includes "Humor and Pathos in Travel," "The Old Virginia Darkey," "Spain – an illustrated travel log," "Our Neighbors Back Door Yard," and "The Making of a Man."

Invitation Dance: given by the Georke Piano company at Mack's Hall last night had 150 invitations issued. The music was furnished by automatic electric pianos.

One event that captured the minds of Colorado City was the giving away of a baby at the Idle Hour Theatre. The Idle Hour was known for giving away prizes as a way to stimulate business at the theatre. In 1910 they hit many headlines when they promoted an "infant" as a prize. Offering a human infant was advertised on many occasions. On the evening of the event people were turned away because so many wanted to attend. The May 27, 1910 issue of *The Argus* reported the giveaway:

There was an air of mystery surrounding the infant, which was kept in the background. Many applied for it, under certain conditions. As far as could be learned, it was a healthy white one, an orphan, whose parents had met violent death in Colorado Springs...that would not be awarded to anyone under eighteen years of age and must be able to guarantee a good home.

H.L. DeMoss of the Brown Palace restaurant was the winner. He was required to answer certain questions relative to the keeping of the infant. The paper reported some alarm was felt for the safety of the baby. The Daughters of Pocahontas, one of the towns secret societies, aided in what *The Argus* deemed as an awful spectacle by some even though it allowed for an orphan to get a home. Funds were raised for the new family to be supplied with milk, bottles and other requirements for a baby.

Mr. Kohn, the owner of the Idle Hour Theatre, stated in an article in April, prior to the giveaway, that he wanted to keep up interest in his business and he had given away almost everything else.

Even today this seems like a strange event for a town that was changing from the wild west days to the responsible workingman's and family man's town.

Cleaning-up Colorado City, 1910 – 1913

L iquor, the question of wet or dry, was a debate that lasted a long time for our nation. Reading the newspapers from that period shows the issue of prohibition was one of the most often written about subjects. Years before Colorado City voted for prohibition, it was a topic of multiple articles.

> Ma is dry, an' Pa is wet,
> Home is horribly upset;
> Pa says temperance is bum,
> Ma attacks the Demon Run,
> Pulls his ears, an' twists his nose,
> Talking of the drunkard's woes,
> Calls the wets a lot of soaks,
> Pa gets mad until he chokes,
> Biggest family ruckus yet;
> Ma is dry, an' Pa is wet. - The Voice *The Argus* 12/1/1911

In the city limits of Colorado Springs, Colorado City's neighbor to the east, it was illegal to sell a drop of alcohol. Prohibition didn't stop the residents from drinking, however, they found many ways to imbibe, and traveling to Colorado City was one. The years leading up the final vote to go dry in Colorado City had many heated debates between its citizens. They also debated the question of the Red-Light District that went hand in hand with drinking. Below is a front page headline found in *The Iris*:

TWO SIDES TO THE STORY/EMPTY STORES EMPTY HOUSES

During the first part of April, 1910, citizens were concerned that numerous houses were empty in Colorado City and these concerns were reported in the paper. The advocates for keeping liquor in the city reported it would raise greater problems for the economy if bars were closed, as there would be twenty more empty store fronts on Colorado Avenue along with lack of tenants for homes.

Those who wanted liquor gone argued that there were many empty businesses already, along with empty houses because families didn't want to live in Colorado City due to its reputation. The arguments went back and forth with *The Iris* supporting prohibition's arguments as follows:

> *Empty houses in the best residence districts and occupied shacks along the tracks and in undesirable parts of town is the rule when saloons hold forth.*
>
> *Colorado City will continue to have hard times just as long as it is content to have about twenty liquor-selling leeches sucking the very life out of her veins.*

One article pointed the remedy for filling empty houses:

REASON: Money that should be spent for home making goes to the rum seller and families of drinking men invariably live in poor houses.

REMEDY: Remove the open saloons and thousands of dollars now worse than wasted will be available for rental for better houses, for groceries, milk, and meat, for clothes and commodities which every family need.

MORAL: Vote against the saloon and for a dry city and you vote for dollars for the property owners, for better business for our merchants and increased comforts for the families of our working men.

Ironically, one interesting article pointed out that it would be nice if Colorado Springs went wet in the coming election and Colorado City went dry, because, the writer reasoned, that for Colorado City:

We could look down upon Colorado Springs in holy horror and point the finger of scorn at them as they have done toward us in the past.

Were things so terrible in Colorado City and not in Colorado Springs? In one *Iris* editorial stated the following:

It was even whispered in this town that druggists over there (Colorado Springs) *sold liquor at the soda fountains by the drink if one knew how to give the proper wink or the true open sesame even in the good old license times. It was this fact that caused a large decrease in the receipts of the open saloons in this city* (Colorado City) *at the time, which had always been supported and kept up on a large degree by the Colorado Springs people.*

Liquor and debauchery went hand and hand, or so one side said. *The Iris* reported this story regarding the Red-Light District quoting the *El Paso County Democrat* of January 29, 1910:

There is an amusing story going around the press and whether or not it is fact, but a flock of buzzards were seen hovering around certain brick houses on Washington Street, (the houses of ill repute of Laura Bell and Mamie Majors) *but when these scavengers came within 1,000 feet of the buildings, they at once clutched their beaks and flew southerly to the chlorination mills in search of better air. And yet the city council of Colorado City compels police officers to enter these vile dens monthly and collect tribute from their wretched inmates and all to save God fearing citizens a few dollars of taxes.*

Also reported in *The Iris* was the headline "How Others See US." The article reported a well-known woman was traveling the state and talking about Colorado City. During one talk the woman gave to over 600 people she said of a visit to Colorado City:

Last evening, I visited Colorado City to see for myself what conditions existed there. I went to the red-light district in the very heart of the city and entered the brothels to investigate. I found the worst reports were not exaggerated. The places were full of fallen girls and men were there in large numbers. What seemed the most terrible feature of all was the presence of so many young men, some were mere boys!

On April 15, 1910, the center article of the front page of *The Iris* featured the headline, "Why Did Not Colorado City Do Its Own Cleaning Up?" The article reported that the new city officials were doing nothing to clean up the Red-Light District. City officials went back and forth each election on the wet/dry issue, each time changing if a blind eye would be enforced in regulating the Red-Light District. One previous administration of Mr. Foote placed a ban on the Red-Light District for the city to dissolve its partnership with prostitution and refused to raise revenue for paying city officials or improving the streets with money from prostitution. With new city officials, it took something else to clean up the District:

> *Then it seemed that providence lent a hand, and by fire purified this unholy district and, in a night, wiped the buildings off the face of the earth.*

The Article continued saying that no sooner had the new officers held up their hands and taken the oath of office to support the laws of the land that Laura Bell:

> *The oldest and most influential sinner of them all, started a brick building said to cost $10,000!*

Mamie Majors, once sentenced to six months in county jail and later pardoned by the Governor on the plea that she had reformed, according to the report:

> *Fitted up the old City Hotel and opened up the house in full blast.*

The Iris reported that everybody noticed great growth and improvement in buildings in a certain part of the city, except Mayor Armstrong and the City Council. The big question of the day was reported in *The Iris*:

> *Since the police magistrate's docket shows that these brazen offenders were dividing their ill-gotten gains with the city each month and were loyally and gracefully helping to carry on the*

financial burdens of the city government (this money seemed to be needed for grading our streets, building sewers, improving our cemetery and for paying the salaries of the city officials), were the city officials participant criminals in the matter? Banish the thought that they, too, might be arrested!

Also noted at the end of the article:

The Iris was edited by the Special Committee in charge of the publicity end of the Anti-saloon campaign, as is plainly evidenced by the subject matter presented.

Who was this Special Committee and why were they in charge of editing the newspaper? It became clearer when a box appeared in *The Iris* which stated:

ATTENTION!
This week's issue of The Iris
is edited by the
Publicity Committee of the
Anti-Saloon Forces.

The Anti-Saloon League was formed in 1904 with Charles L. Cunningham of Colorado City as its first president. It adopted a constitution stating the members of the league were not of any political party and would not participate in politics but focus on agitation, legislation and law enforcement in the effort to suppress saloons.

Nationwide the Anti-Saloon League was a lobbying organization founded in the late 1800s, larger than the Women's Christian Temperance Union and the Prohibition Party. Colorado City had a very active chapter and published their newsletter called *The Anti-Saloon Advocate*.

Headlines in the *El Paso County Democrat* reported things were looking up regarding cleaning up the county. The headlines read "The Lawless Element Must Reform and Move On."

> *The lawless element of the community, if wise, will reform or move on. It no longer cuts any figure in politics. No man with a grain of political power wants the support of the tottering saloon power. Time was when the saloons and dives and tin horns held the balance of power in this county. Thank God that day has passed. Without political pull criminals are utterly helpless. Two towns in the county still have saloons, but they are DOOMED! …Those who cannot reconcile themselves to the changed order of things can move on to Nevada, Arizona and New Mexico. Colorado has outgrown frontier methods and manners. Without reference to party, all good citizens will, must, uphold the District Judges, the Sheriff, District Attorney and other officials who are forwarding the movement to redeem this county from the scourge of harlotism.*

The Baptist church was front and center in the fight to clean up Colorado City. There was a movement at the time for anti-liquor groups to hold meetings at different churches around Colorado City. The headline "FIRST BIG GUNS FIRED FOR A "DRY" TOWN" was the center front story on February 3, 1910 of *The Iris* and announced the Union Anti-Saloon meeting at the Baptist Church.

The Iris reported again on the Baptist Church in its April 29, 1910 paper. It stated a packed house greeted Rev. Willard McCarthy at the Union Meeting. The pastor won laurels from the audience at the Baptist church. The subject of the lecture was "Have Saloons Benefited Colorado City."

It was reported that the audience was alert during every minute as the lecturer spoke in generalities but every blow struck home. With local color, and a dramatic setting down of a little brown jug, together with the speaker's droll Irish wit and earnest talk, he enforced his argument to the people for a "dry" town, reported *The Iris*. Even if those who attended might not agree with the speaker's views; it was a lecture that would be remembered. The pastors of most of the churches of Colorado City were on the platform with the speaker with Rev. Turnbull of the Baptist church presiding. It was regretted that so many did not get inside the doors of the church. It was the purposes of the ministers to have these meetings reach all parts of the city rather than to centralize them in one church reported *The Iris*.

A letter to the Editor of *The Iris* was also printed in the April edition on the front page from the Rev. Frank Hullinger of Craig, Colorado, who owned property in Colorado City. He commended the positive stand taken by *The Iris* for good order and decency. He wrote he never believed in the financial argument that it was necessary to have the revenue from sink holes of iniquity to carry the town. He stated that most citizens are not willing to *be partners in crime with the most revolting characters.*

SAM SMALL

Friday Night, January 6th

8 O'CLOCK

The Methodist Episcopal Church

Corner of Third Street and Lincoln Avenue

Under auspices of the Colorado City Ministerial Assoc

"Civic Righteousness and Liquor Legislation"

With quotations from his famous lecture on

"His Satanic Majesty the Devil"

Public Invited, no charge for admission

Silver offering after the Address.

ENOUGH SAID! - Advertizement - Colorado City Iris

The April edition of *The Iris* carried the headline "Saloons Serve as Fuel for Red-Light District" in yet another article against saloons. The article reported in a recent raid on the Red-Light District by El Paso County, saloon men rushed over to the county jail to bail out the twenty-four women arrested:

> *Whenever saloons exist then social evils flourish, and when Colorado City puts her saloons out of business the Red light District, as a natural result, will be no more and the inmates of these houses will steal away to the towns with saloons to abide.*

Also reported was that women from Colorado Springs did not come to Colorado City to shop. Women did the buying of groceries, clothing and household furnishings. They spend ten dollars to every dollar a man spends on maintaining a home. It was hurting the business of Colorado City merchants who brought honest revenue to Colorado City.

The headline "Five Red-Light Women Fined" was the center front page article in the May 27, 1910 edition of *The Iris*. They reported that a fine of $25 and costs were levied against Nellie White, Rosie Paxton, Mamie Majors, Eula Hames and Laura Bell of Colorado City in district court after they had pled guilty of conducting disorderly houses in the Red-Light District. Colorado City might just fine these ladies, but there was the law of El Paso County to follow too. Before the sentence was passed, El Paso County Assistant District Attorney Purcell informed the court:

> *That so far as his office was concerned, he was not disposed to be severe on the defendants in the present prosecution, but he wanted it distinctly understood that the policy of his office was to have the Redlight District in Colorado City closed as he believed the majority of the residents there were in favor of such termination.*

The women were represented by Attorneys Kinsley and Lombard and the City Attorney of Colorado City, John Watt. On behalf of their clients, Kinsley answered Purcell to the effect that it was an open question as to whether the majority of Colorado City residents wanted the houses closed.

By June of 1910 Colorado City's two sides continued to fight over the wet or dry issue. Below are the cries from both sides of the issue:

You will kill the town if the saloons shut.

No town has died or been permanently hurt due to going dry.

In *The Iris* article of June 17, 1910 the paper reported the position of the dry side:

> *We do not claim that the saloon keepers and the brewery men and the gamblers and the harlots now in town will not suffer, but are they the city? We claim the city will not suffer if the saloons go. The interest in the 70 persons engaged in the saloon business is less that the interest of the 5,000 people in the city.*

Those in favor of going dry argued that there was $250,000 a year spent on liquor that would be better spent in other channels:

> *First take the man away from the saloon. Second, take the saloon away from the man.*

In many ways the supporters of the saloons were right about the town being hurt. The four main houses in the Red-Light District, it was reported, were shown on the Police Magistrate's Docket Records to have paid $1,140 in fines in the last five months of 1909. Each house had to pay $25 per month and $10 for each "lady" kept. City and State laws forbade licenses issued for houses of ill repute to run, so fines were issued and laws were evaded. Reported in *The Iris*:

> *What is the paltry sum of the fines compared to the disgrace and blot upon the name of our city, and the moral ruin and degradation of our sons and daughters? Away with such blood money. It will pollute our city. The stench of their pollution is borne on every wind and the injury to city must be borne by the innocent.*

Ironically after the vote to go dry one headline would read, "Colorado City Cash Box Nearly Empty" and it was reported that the city had never been so broke in its history.

As the debate continued, many argued for larger license fees for saloons. The thought was, there would be less drinking if there were fewer saloons that could pay the license fee. Below is a letter to the Editor of *The Iris*:

> *Editor – I once lived in a town near here having twelve saloons. They paid three hundred twenty-five dollars license each. A move started by the temperance people to get the license raised to two thousand dollars each. To their surprise, four or five of the leading "saloon men" began to work for it by speeches and offers of money and their argument was like this: 'Four or five of us can pay this fee and make more money than at present if we can close the other places.' For saloon men are humans when it comes to profits. Neither are they shedding any tears of love and sympathy over each other. Saloon men are always closely united when it comes to protection but ready to knife each other for profit. There are three or four saloon men*

in Colorado City who would pay any license for a monopoly of the business. Now how about the argument that if we had fewer saloons we would be taking advance grounds. The saloon men favor this move, Respectfully, A. Reader

Following that letter was an article talking about James Rumsey who was being charged with selling liquor to several minors. Prior to his hearing he was granted a liquor license so that he could conduct a saloon in Colorado City, pending the outcome of his court case. Rumsey was convicted and paid a fine for serving liquor to minors. The question asked in the article was, "What action would council take; would he keep his license?"

It was reported at a meeting of city council on September 9, 1910 under the headlines "City Cannot Thrive on Revenue from Saloons:"

We can't depend upon the revenue of the saloons and objectionable houses for public improvements.

The Iris reported that nothing was truer:

Let us be men and go down in our pocket, in an honest way, and pay the taxes required to support our city and not try to shirk our duty by going into the league with the liquor business to cause some poor drunkard or fallen women to pay our bills for us.

Some agreed it was not good to run a city on money from liquor and prostitution but argued the following:

Why should man need a guardian to tell him what to eat or drink. Both high class men and working men have weak among them. There will always be drunks but most men should not have to have their good qualities judged by others bad qualities. Men should not be deprived of their liberties.

Some felt it was better to keep the drinking in one section of town than illegally hid all over the town. Overall, thoughts were changing to favor the opinion liquor and all that surrounded the consumption of liquor was evil. The following poem was printed in the paper and supported the growing opinion against saloons:

The Bar
Bar – that is true,
A bar to heaven, a door to hell,
Whoever named it named it well.
A bar to manliness and wealth,
A door to want and broken health.
A bar to hope a bar to prayer,
A door to darkness and despair.
A bar to honored useful life,
A door to frowning senseless strife.
A bar to all that is true and brave,
A door to every drunkards grave.
A bar to joys that home imparts,
A door to tears and aching hearts.
A bar to heaven a door to hell,
Whoever named in named it well.
Unknown 1910 in Colo. City Iris

What was to come was inevitable. Churches, unions, newspapers and women's groups called for prohibition. The Women's Christian Temperance Union urged that measures be brought out for the fall election for the entire State of Colorado. A circular letter was issued by the W.C.T.U.:

> Now is the time to prepare for the submission of a prohibitory amendment by the legislators elected this fall. It will be two years before it can be voted on by the people. If it is not submitted this winter it postpones the possibility of prohibition for four more years...It will also allow Colorado to become the dumping ground for the outlawed brewer, distiller and saloon keeper from her neighboring states...believing this measure would result in safety to childhood, honor to manhood and womanhood and glory to our beloved state, we bespeak your careful, prayerful consideration and decision.

A vote in 1911 for Colorado City to go dry would be argued in court with only a few votes separating the outcome and each side saying there was voter fraud. Plans were in progress for hindrances to be placed in the way if the outcome favored prohibition. Boot-legging and all other forms of illegally selling and evading the law were expected. The formation of a new city north on Fourth Street outside of city limits was being planned. It was reported that a number of saloon men and wholesale liquor dealers were ready to begin construction in the new town, only a few blocks away from downtown Colorado City, if the court case did not turn in their favor. Planned for the town were a vaudeville theatre, a baseball park, a barber shop, a restaurant and a hotel. In the April 5, 1912 edition of *The Iris* the headlines read "All Liquor Licenses Renewed; Much Routine." The number of saloons in Colorado City was falling. Only eight were remaining. One year later

Colorado City would officially go dry in April of 1913.

The new town of Ramona was formed just a few blocks north of Colorado Avenue up Fourth Street, around today's Uintah and 24th Street. Alcohol still flowed. *The Anti-Saloon Advocate* was still published in Colorado City knowing the city was known for turning a blind eye on liquor laws. An article in the *Advocate* titled "First Victory Won – Colorado City Dry – Line Up for the Second Battle" pointed out the following:

> *The paramount issue is now to elect officers to enforce local option law. Do we want to make a farce of it by letting the old gang get in again to put in police officers who will wink at violations of law and blind pigs, blind tigers, clubs and boot-leggers to flourish?*

The article went on to say of Colorado City's police force:

> *They couldn't even discover a blind elephant if it was in the middle of the grass growing on the streets.*

The Anti-Saloon League pushed to elect only those who would insure Colorado City would be physically and legally dry. The March 1913 issue of *The Anti-Saloon Advocate* pointed out that good upstanding businesses, family business, saw an increase in their sales within the first 25 days of going dry. Revenue Colorado City received from saloon licensing did not bring in the needed revenue for the city to prosper. Good businesses, in a town where a family would be proud to live, were in the long run a better way to prosper. The battle was still being waged and Mack's Hall was still holding meetings every night for the Anti-Saloon League. One quote from their newsletter hits home even today for some people. With the benefits of the revenue received today from legalized marijuana, the rise in homelessness on our streets and the growing deaths from drug overdoses, the words of yesterday still ring today:

> *Should these revenues – wages of iniquity – be put into the treasury? They are the price of blood, and in their aggregate would be inadequate to buy fields enough to bury the multitudes who are the victims of the dreadful (liquor) traffic. - Anti Saloon League*

Ramona

All Hail Colorado City! Dry by a 104-vote majority!
The Iris 1913

N o sooner had the vote for prohibition in Colorado City passed
in 1913, the fight began to stop the new town of Ramona from
becoming the next haven for liquor. On June 6, 1913, *The Iris* ran with
the center front headlines:

Forces are Lining Up for Battle Against Liquor in the New Town...
Owner of the Colorado Springs Newspaper
Will Lead the Attack on Rum

The Iris reported the *El Paso County Democrat*, controlled by Judge
Louis Cunningham, stated Cunningham would be looking after the
dry fences and will thwart the plans of Ramona to run as an open
town. The *El Paso County Democrat* stated that a pledge to raise $5,000
toward the cause of making all of El Paso County dry had been made
by Cunningham.

By September *The Argus* was reporting a monster mass meeting
held at the Temple Theatre concerning the Ramona matter. Colorado
Springs invited the citizens of Colorado City, all church members

and good citizens to attend a meeting to discuss plans for stopping the "moral cesspool" from being in their midst. The City Council of Colorado Springs had unanimously passed a motion not to allow mains or tabs for water to be placed in Ramona.

While the fight was ongoing, the town of Ramona began to feature its attraction of holding prize fights, deemed by the newspaper as a most disgraceful affair that should be stopped by the Sheriff. *The Argus* described brutal fights, disguised as boxing matches, as terrible beatings occurring under the nose of the Sheriff. Drunks wandered into Colorado City and took time and money in the police courts when arrested. The article warned Sheriff Birdsall that if he wanted to be reelected, he would take note of this problem.

On October 30, 1914, the headline read "Where was Birdsell When the Lights Went Out?" *The Argus* reported on Ramona:

> *The prize fight at Ramona Tuesday night wound up in a regular knock down and drag out in which the audience took its hand and decorated each other with black eyes, bloody noses, swollen faces and disturbed tempers.*

A call by a referee was not liked by the crowd and a fight began with the natural outcome of liquor and lack of law. Where was Birdsall? He was dressed up and attending a Commercial Club banquet trying to get votes. Also stated in the article:

> *The District Attorney was at home in bed dreaming of another term in office, drawing a big salary for himself and son and fooling people into the belief that he is a good officer, which he is not.*
>
> *The paper has maintained that these prize fights are a disgrace to this county, that they are in violation of the state law and it is*

the duty of the officers, Sheriff Birdsell and Mike Purcell to arrest and prosecute them.

The newspaper reported Birdsall and Purcell would not do anything because the businessmen of Ramona knew too much about the way Birdsall and Purcell did business and managed their offices but there would come a time when the "gang" that stood behind them, some in high places, would be gone. It was reported that Birdsall and seven of his deputies arrived at Ramona when the fight broke out, after leaving the banquet. Although Birdsall was there, no arrests were made.

It should be notice that Sheriff Birdsall's name had previously appeared in the paper spelled with an 'a' until the battle for prohibition got heated. It can then be noted that *The Argus* spelled the name with an 'e'. *The Argus* did use nicknames for those they disagreed with and the spelling could be a mistake or a way to show that he 'sold out' bending an eye to corruption.

In January 22, 1915, an editorial appeared using the new name *The Argus* had given the District Attorney, "Fog Horn Mike." The editorial pointed out that Purcell was pushing for the Sheriff in Cripple Creek to clean up their town and the editorial pointed out that not a day went by that the law was not violated in Ramona.

It was not just Ramona that was under fire. When Colorado City went dry, the push for even more reform occurred. The push for all business to be closed on Sundays began, hitting close to home for many of the family owned businesses such as the theatre. Name calling and finger pointing on who was or was not a good Christian appeared in editorials. Colorado City's division was growing deeper.

Ramona didn't start out to be a controversial place. As early as 1910 lots in the new Ramona Addition were advertised. A contest was held to promote families to move to Ramona by the real estate office of Kinsman & Wolff of 404 Colorado Avenue. A full-page spread appeared in *The Argus* on June 6, 1910 stating two lots would be given to the person who was successful in forming the greatest number of words from the statement "Ramona Acres Tracts and Lots."

All words would have to be in a numbered list, in ink. Words must be from a Webster dictionary no earlier than 1886. Proper names could not be used. No letters could be repeated any more than they were found in the sentence. Any list with over fifty errors would be rejected. The list must be in alphabetical order and submitted by September 1, 1910.

People lived in Ramona prior to Colorado City going dry. The July 7, 1911 edition of *The Argus* presented an article on the splendid Ramona gardens. Robert McReynolds, living in Ramona, was growing a surprisingly wonderful garden. Not normally a farmer, but with energy, moisture and the good soil, he was growing the following vegetables:

...beets that beat'em all; lettuce that beats the deuce; onions that are warm numbers; beans that need poling to keep them from running away; turnips that excel.

The Dairy Ramona advertised in the paper. Located on North Fourth Street, owners Fretz and Lewis sold only *strictly pure milk, cream and buttermilk.* They asked residents to patronize their home industry and promised prompt service.

Sadly, the town would get a bad name after Colorado City voted to go dry. Remembering Ramona fifty years later on January 13, 1963, it was reported in *The Colorado Springs Gazette*:

At any rate, Colorado City was dry and the new town of Ramona came to life with a vengeance. Old accounts say that the wet interest moved bodily to the new town, asked the State for a charter, organized a council and mayor type of government and after a fashion, were prepared to prosper.

And prosper they did! The place roared, so much so that according to accounts of the times, not only was it not safe for a decent woman to be seen there, but even a man alone at night was very likely to end up with a lump on his head and his pockets empty.

The town of Ramona was short lived. Formed to allow the sale of alcohol when Colorado City voted for prohibition, the original purpose for the founding of the town would not last for long. The State of Colorado voted for prohibition just a few years later. The following editorial appeared in 1916 in *The Colorado City Independent* showing the desired future of the town:

THE PASSING OF RAMONA

No more will the musician sit before the piano at Ramona and tickle the ivories, while men line up before the bar and keep time with the clink of glasses. No more will Colorado City officials be required to spend most of their time at the corner of Fourth and Colorado Avenue to act as a steering committee to pass the booze-soaked hides on down the line to Colorado Springs. The oasis has vanished from the desert and the thirsty souls must go to greener pastures or be satisfied with water. Crepe was tied on the doors up there last Friday night, and Ramona passed into lost cities of the country.

Now the people up there can settle down to peace and quiet, can boost and boom that location as a beautiful residence site, a place for homes, where scenery and beauty are before the eyes at all times, for this location commands the best view of the mountains to be had in the entire district.

Colorado City can fix up the beautiful little park again and our people can go up there with the knowledge that they will not be disturbed.

Ramona should be a part of the city and it likely will in time, for the people of this town are going to take an interest in the welfare of her people that they never took before. They are going to paint their houses, beautify the lawns, the parking and the streets with flowers to make a garden spot here that people will delight to see and Ramona will fall into line and do the same.

Perhaps you do not know it but there are a lot of new faces in this town; people who are coming here because this city is and has been clean, because it will be a good place to raise a family and to build a home.

The Town of Romona pictured in 1914, looking north from todays 24th Street, now where Thorndale Park is located.
(OCCHS Archives, McKnight Collection)

One of the sad effects of the battle to go dry both in Colorado City and

Ramona was many town people who were friends, no longer were. *The Iris* in an editorial in March of 1915 pointed out people would no longer shop at certain stores, as the owner had backed the opposite side of the prohibition question. This was bad for all businesses and for the town. The editor pointed out:

> This paper is and has been opposed to the policies of George Gieger and Byron Hames in regard to their Ramona enterprises, yet we like both of them personally and would go out of our way to do them a favor. Because we believe one way and them another is no reason why we cannot be friends in a business way and as neighbors. Forget it folks, lay aside those petty prejudices and get down to business and boost for this city.

Too much had been said against too many people who were against prohibition to pull the city together. After multiple years of printing stories on the evils of alcohol, town folks were not getting along. *The Iris* changed their tune, trying to pull the city together, but it was too little too late:

> What is the matter with Colorado City? Have the people of this town gone to sleep and left the care of their good city to providence, or have they taken it upon themselves to knock every other person in the town; to kill it with their own talk? This good old town has not lost all of its self-respect, neither have the people given up in despair.
>
> But honestly, there are more wall eyed, sore headed damphool knockers to the square inch here, than any other place on the face of the earth...the town was in as bad shape before the saloons were closed as it is now, or worse...Trade at home. Boost the town.

Unfortunately, the following poem, author unknown, printed in the March 20, 1915 edition of *The Iris* shows the long slow slide that divided Colorado City and the last attempts to pull it back:

It's Not Your Town, It's You
If you want to live in the kind of town
Like the kind of town you like,
You need NOT slip your clothes in a grip
And start on a long, long hike,
You'll only find what you left behind
For there is nothing that's really new,
It's a knock at yourself when you knock your town,
It is not you town – it's you.

Colorado City – No More

First to go was liquor, next was Colorado City. We know the outcome; the people of Colorado City endorsed annexation on a rainy day in April, 1917. *The Iris* headlines "Colorado City – No More" reported of the 1,099 people who registered their choice in the matter, 638 voted for annexation while 461 voted against:

> *Although the weather man dished up a brand of weather that would ordinarily be expected to dampen the ardor of the most enthusiastic worker for or against any position, he failed to stay the hosts who were battling for Annexation of Colorado City to Colorado Springs.*

What were the thoughts of the people of Colorado City prior to the monumental decision to "be no more?" In December of 1915, a little over one year before the vote, and with the new year of 1916 approaching, *The Iris* started rumbling of things to come. Reported in the front page an editorial printed on New Year's Eve:

> *What will the New Year mean to Colorado City, tomorrow*

another year is before us. The last one was a short but eventful one, not alone for the people of the world, but for Colorado City as well. The future lies before us that we may make of it just what we please, a booming city, or a dead hole, pointed at with scorn by the other towns of the state, or with pride.

The editorial went on to say that Colorado City was better financially than ever before, even better than when the saloons were in town. Colorado City had the Midland railroad, the largest payroll in the county, and the Golden Cycle Mill. Both employed many men who all spent money on the smaller businesses in the town. The article urged the people of Colorado City to stop grumbling that Colorado City was dead and ended with the following:

WHY FOLKS, COLORADO CITY IS THE LIVELIEST OLD MULE IN THE LAND AND SHE HAS A KICK WITH A PUNCH TO IT. GET THAT IN YOUR MIND.

Although the editorial on the front page suggested that Colorado City was not on the way out, just six months prior another front-page article in *The Iris* differed. The article discussed people of Colorado City who bragged about the city being debt free and proud, were wrong. *The Iris* suggested that a city that was out of debt and had no plans for debt was not growing. In towns that were growing, taxes were increased and debt was planned. This allowed for new schools and roads for more families and businesses. It suggested the old Bancroft building be moved, that parks should be planned, a fine High School should be built, streets should be paved and Colorado Avenue should be a blaze of lights from one end to another.

Since the vote to go dry in Colorado City, those who were for prohibition were so involved proving that Colorado City would not go in debt due to the lack of revenue from the sale of alcohol, they put the lack of debt above growth and improvements. Colorado City was not dead, but it was surely stagnant. By December of 1916 a proposed city ordinance was submitted stating the terms and conditions of the Commissioners concerning a proposed annexation of Colorado City to Colorado Springs. Colorado City would turn over all of its assets and property. All of Colorado City's debt would be paid by Colorado Springs. After annexation, Colorado City would receive equal police department, health, sanitation, fire protection and water supply as Colorado Springs. Colorado Springs would maintain and continue Colorado City's library and cemetery. All licenses issued by Colorado City for businesses would be honored by Colorado Springs. The terms and salaries of any Colorado City officers and employees would cease and they must seek election or appointment of positions as a resident of Colorado Springs. The next year would be one of debate before the citizens would vote on the fate of Colorado City.

Those who were against annexation felt nothing would be gained, as Colorado City already had the same amenities as Colorado Springs; lights, gas, water, street cars. Their argument was it was better to rent water from the Colorado Springs Water Works rather than to take on the immense bonded indebtedness that Colorado Springs had along with the cost of upkeep and improvements.

Another argument against annexation was, Colorado City was out of debt and its tax revenue covered what was needed, while Colorado Springs was in debt. Concern was voiced regarding the burdens being placed on property owners of Colorado City to cover the debt of Colorado Springs and having to give up the water rights valued at about $50,000 that Anthony Bott had generously donated to Colorado City.

It was also noted that Colorado City employees worked for low salaries and Colorado Springs was, according to reports in the paper:

Woefully extravagant, burdened with high salaries and numerous employees always clamoring for more money.

There was great concern that the Colorado City business center, which did have vacancies due to the outlawing of saloons, would become even less important, causing an increase in empty buildings.

Finally, it was argued that while it was wonderful to want to be part of the "great" Colorado Springs, they had a higher cost of living. Colorado City residents should show patriotism for their beautiful city in the nicest location. Those who did not want annexation felt Colorado City had gone through a cleaning up with prohibition and was well on the way to seeing a better day without Colorado Springs.

The Colorado City Independent, formerly *The Iris,* was pro annexation and throughout the first few months of 1917 ran a series of articles entitled "Why We Should Annex." As usual, *The Argus* reported the news and did not take a stance on annexation, for or against, although they often mentioned that it was *The Iris* that caused so much division in Colorado City by their over zealous statements against businessmen with establishments that allowed drinking. *The* Argus was very clear on what they believed would be the demise of Colorado City and wrote in 1912:

Experience has shown that the best way to kill a town is to legislate against liberty. Very few people now-a-days believe in wide-open towns, but many are opposed to moves that tend to kill a town as the modern 'blue laws' do. A man can be coaxed to church, but cannot be driven...Colorado has been badly inured by some non-progressive people of the rule or ruin policy along these lines.

The Argus pointed out to be careful in a vote for annexation, as if done, it could never be undone. Although they did say being annexed might be good, by getting rid of the name Colorado City that the Iris man (what they called the editor of *The Iris*) had so often spoken ill about in the paper. *The Argus* felt it remained to be seen if annexation would be beneficial but it might be a good way to end the division in Colorado City. They believed that the Iris man was the cause for much of Colorado City's division.

Those against annexation felt that fire insurance for properties would be greater if Colorado City became part of Colorado Springs. *The Independent* covered this topic in February of 1917 stating that rates for insurance were made by the Rocky Mountain Fire Underwriters Association of Denver. The article compared rates on properties built with like kind materials and equal hazard areas and found that rates would not be increased; in fact, rates were lower in Colorado Springs. Rates were based on water pressure and supply. Colorado City was paying more than Colorado Springs. If annexation occurred, residents would have the ability to complain to the city to make payment the same as Colorado Springs.

In late January of 1917 the Annexation Club was organized. Its executive committee was G. Birdsall, G. Gilmore and C. Sheetz. Talks were held and plans were outlined for a vigorous campaign based on facts and figures to insure annexation. Advertisements were placed in the papers in support of this issue:

WHERE THERE'S UNITY
THERE IS STRENGTH!

The people of the Pikes Peak Region have one common end in view – the building of a bigger and better Community. Those favoring Annexation truly believe that the first great step in that direction is the Unity of government, and a brotherly feeling among all the people of the region. Join in the great movement tending to that end.

In the two months leading up to the vote, articles appeared summing up the reason *The Colorado City Independent* was in favor of annexation. The ten-point summary of those articles came out a few days before the election:

First – Colorado City pays more than they should for insurance.

Second – Colorado City pays more than 25% more in taxes that Colorado Springs.

Third – Colorado City gains more worth by being part owner in the water plant than it takes on in debt maintaining the plant.

Fourth – Colorado City's post office will already be a sub-station of Colorado Springs as of July 1917.

Fifth – Annexation will allow Colorado City to become a terminal rate point.

Sixth – Schools will be still run as they are and those who questioned changes due to annexation no longer are debating this issue.

Seventh – The citizens of Colorado City will reap the benefits derived from the thoroughly organized Department of Health and Sanitation which is composed of Commissioner, Market Master, Inspector of Weights and Measures, Public School Nurses, Plumbing Inspector, Chemist and Bacteriologist.

Eighth – Annexation will not entail extra expenses on property owners

Ninth – Colorado City will become residents of one of the foremost cities of the state, a city known in all parts of America.

Tenth – You will be part of the County Capital of El Paso and you can take your visiting friends to show them the Court House, City Hall, Burns Opera House, The National Printers Home, the State institution for the Deaf and Blind, Bethel, St. Francis and Glockner hospitals, the Antlers and other fine hotels, the Federal Post Office, the Mining Exchange, the Exchange National and many other financial businesses and Colorado College.

The Independent took a strong stance for annexation:

> *The Independent feels that it has stood up for Colorado City in this campaign. Not, perhaps for the NAME, but for what it has honestly thought was for the best interest of the PEOPLE. It has tried to forget sentimentalism and deal with the question in a cold-blooded business manner. Sentiment will not pay taxes, nor insurance, nor buy bread and butter. With these few remarks we pass the question up for final judgment by the voters next Tuesday, and wish to thank you one and all for your kind forbearance.*

The Colorado City Independent became the *Colorado Springs Independent* in June of 1917 and reported Colorado City's ending:

> *With the first crowing of the cock on Monday morning the old historic town of Colorado City yielded its identity and the territory embraced within its limits and became a suburban part of Colorado Springs. Let the spirit of friendship and fellowship have full sway!*

Epilogue

Colorado City is now the west side of Colorado Springs. Its independent attitude and pride of community still exists. Things still are changing, as they always will. Today traveling down Colorado Avenue can be found numerous places to obtain an alcoholic drink. No more are groups like the Women's Christian Temperance Union persuading people to make a pledge of sobriety. Many of our modern "watering holes" hold some of the finest restaurants to be found in Colorado. Wine bars, martini bars, Greek, Mexican, French and Italian food, breakfast, lunch and dinner, tapas and the best buffalo chili can all be found.

One thing new in the last few years is the number of places where marijuana is sold. Since the legalization of marijuana, the west side has become a place for many homeless people to camp. Just like at the turn of the century, discussion is often heard by local businessmen and residents regarding the problem vagrants cause with tourist trade, business and safety. Today the city does not require people "capable of working" not loiter in the streets as they did in Colorado City. Colorado City ordinances required compliance to the no loitering ordinance, or leave the area. The city is once again divided. One side thinks to be compassionate, people should choose the lifestyle they desire, allowing people to live on the streets. The other side see the destruction of businesses and infringements on the rights of those who don't want people sleeping or pan handling on the streets. They believe it is compassionate to remove vagrants from the street and find ways to help them to a better life.

When I was growing up in the early 70s, before the revitalization of Old Colorado City occurred, many of the store fronts were empty and the west side was run down; beautiful historic buildings were crumbling. Let us hope that history doesn't repeat itself. Colorado City, now the west side of Colorado Springs, must work to keep the west side an environment for families of the future.

Bibliography

Aldridge, Dorothy. *Historic Colorado City, the Town with the Future, a Quick History*, Old Colorado City History Center, Colorado Springs, Colorado, 1996.

Anderson, John Wesley. *Rankin Scott Kelly, First Sheriff El Paso County, Colorado Territory*, Old Colorado City Historical Society, Colorado Springs, Colorado, 2017.

Barbaro, Barbara. *Law and Disorder in Colorado City 1859-1917*, Old Colorado City Historical Society, Colorado Springs, Colorado, 2009.

Biographical Record of the State of Colorado, Chapman Publishing Company, Chicago, Illinois, 1898.

Casey, Merv. *West Word, Colorado Opera Houses,* Old Colorado City Historical Society, Colorado Springs, Colorado, 2007.

City Directory of Colorado Springs, Colorado City and Manitou, The Out West Printing and Stationery Company, Colorado Springs, Colorado 1888-1917 editions.

Colorado City Argus, Colorado City, Colorado, various editions.

Colorado City Iris, Colorado City, Colorado, 1889 – 1917 editions.

Colorado Springs Gazette, Colorado Springs, Colorado, various editions.

Dymkoski, Catherine. *West Word, Jacob Schmidt Family History,* Old

Colorado City Historical Society, Colorado Springs, Colorado, 2009.

Easterbrook, Jim. *The Time Traveler in Old Colorado*, Great Western Press, Colorado Springs, Colorado, 1985.

Fosdick, Lucy H., *Across the Plains in '61,* Concord Massachusetts Journal, Concord, Massachusetts, approximate date 1861.

Fossett, Frank, *Colorado Its God and Silver Mines, Farms and Stock Ranges and Health and Pleasure Reports – Tourist's Guide of the Rocky Mountains,* C.G. Cranford, New York, 1879.

Gilman, Nadine. *Hearts of Gold? Colorado Painted Ladies: Who and Why,* Old Colorado City Historical Society, Colorado Springs, Colorado, 2002.

Gordon, Irving L. *U.S. History, Review Text,* Amsco Publications, Logan, IA, 1986.

Griswold, Don and Jean. *Colorado's Century of Cities,* United States, 1958.

Hardy, Roberta. *West Word, Colorado City's Laura Bell McDaniel,* Old Colorado City Historical Society, Colorado Springs, Colorado, August 2016.

Hughes, Dave. *West Word, A Look at Saloons Past,* Old Colorado City Historical Society, Colorado Springs, Colorado, Special Edition.

Hughes, Dave. *West Word, An Original Fosdick Plat Found,* Old Colorado City Historical Society, Colorado Springs, Colorado, 2011.

Hughes, Dave. *West Word, Controversial Charles Stockbridge*, Old Colorado City Historical Society, Colorado Springs, Colorado, 2003.

Hughes, Dave. *West Word, The Fosdicks Across the Plains in '61*, Old Colorado City Historical Society, Colorado Springs, Colorado,

Hughes, Dave. *West Word, Henry Templeton,* Old Colorado City Historical Society, Colorado Springs, Colorado, 2009,

Knox, Jan. *West Word, The Hottest Town on the Front Range – Abstract from the Colorado Springs Independent*, Colorado Springs, Colorado, October 3, 1946.

Knudson, Leo, Suzanne Schorsch, Sharon Swint, *Tunnel Tales of Old Colorado City – Stories of Saloons, Bordellos, Secret Societies and Tunnels*, Old Colorado City Historical Society, Colorado Springs, Colorado, 2018.

MacKell, Jan. *Brothels Bordellos and Bad Girls, Prostitution in Colorado 1860-1930*, University of New Mexico Press, Albuquerque, New Mexico, 2009,

MacKell, Jan. *Red Light Women of the Rocky Mountains*, University of New Mexico Press, Albuquerque, New Mexico, 2009.

Michaels, Lance and Lee. *West Word, Laura Bell McDaniel,* Old Colorado City Historical Society, Colorado Springs, Colorado, 1993.

Norman, Cathleen. *In and Around Old Colorado City, a Walking Tour,* Preservation Publishing for the Old Colorado City Historical Society, Lakewood, Colorado, 2001.

Rocky Mountain Directory and Colorado Gazetteer for 1871, S.S. Wallihan & Company, Denver, Colorado 1871.

Rutter, Michael. *Upstairs Girls, Prostitution in the American West*, Farcountry Press, U.S.A. 2005.

Shepard, Paul. *West Word, Colorado City Strike*, Old Colorado City Historical Society, Colorado Springs, Colorado, 2008.

Schorsch, Suzanne. *West Word, The Gehrung Family and Colorado City*, Old Colorado City Historical Society, Colorado Springs, Colorado 2018.

South Arnold, Karen. *Playing Grandma's Games*, Western Reflections Publishing, Ouray, Colorado, 2000.

Tate, Mary. *Judge Stone, Synopsis, West Word*, Old Colorado City Historical Society, Colorado Springs, Colorado.

Websites
https://en.wikipedia.org/wiki/Knights_of_Pythias
https://en.wikipedia.org/wiki/L._Frank_Baum
https://en.wikipedia.org/wiki/List_of_town_and_city_fires
https://en.wikipedia.org/wiki/Modern_Woodmen_of_America
https://en.wikipedia.org/wiki/Molly_Elliot_Seawell
https://en.wikipedia.org/wiki/Odd_Fellows
http://www.abrahamlincolnonline.org/lincoln/speeches/house.htm
https://www.wctu.org/history.html

www.ingramcontent.com/pod-product-compliance
Lightning Source LLC
Chambersburg PA
CBHW020156090426
42734CB00008B/842